Also by Michael I. Bennett, MD, and Sarah Bennett

*F\*ck Feelings*

# F*ck Love

One Shrink's Sensible Advice
for Finding a Lasting Relationship

## Michael I. Bennett, MD, and Sarah Bennett

**Touchstone**

New York   London   Toronto   Sydney   New Delhi

Touchstone
An Imprint of Simon & Schuster, Inc.
1230 Avenue of the Americas
New York, NY 10020

Copyright © 2017 by FXCK FEELINGS LLC

First Touchstone hardcover edition February 2017

TOUCHSTONE and colophon are registered trademarks of Simon & Schuster, Inc.

For information about special discounts for bulk purchases,
please contact Simon & Schuster Special Sales at 1-866-506-1949
or business@simonandschuster.com.

The Simon & Schuster Speakers Bureau can bring authors to your live event.
For more information or to book an event contact the Simon & Schuster Speakers Bureau
at 866-248-3049 or visit our website at www.simonspeakers.com.

Manufactured in the United States of America

10   9   8   7   6   5   4   3   2   1

Library of Congress Cataloging-in-Publication Data

Names: Bennett, Michael, 1945- author. | Bennett, Sarah (Humorist), author.
Title: F*ck love : one shrink's sensible advice for finding a lasting
   relationship / Michael I. Bennett, MD and Sarah Bennett.
Other titles: Fuck love
Description: New York : Touchstone, [2017] | Includes index.
Identifiers: LCCN 2016037442 (print) | LCCN 2016050552 (ebook) | ISBN
   9781501140563 (hardcover) | ISBN 9781501140570 (eBook)
Subjects: LCSH: Man-woman relationships. | Couples--Psychology. | Sex
   (Psychology) | Interpersonal relations. | Interpersonal communication.
Classification: LCC HQ801 .B4727 2017 (print) | LCC HQ801 (ebook) | DDC
   306.7--dc23
LC record available at https://lccn.loc.gov/2016037442

ISBN 978-1-5011-4056-3
ISBN 978-1-5011-4057-0 (ebook)

## Dedications

*Both Bennetts:* To Mona, wife and mother, co creator of the truth behind this book and anchor of our lives for over forty years/-ever.

*MB:* To Peter Bleiberg, my brother-in-law and better-than-brother.

*SB:* To the man who wrote more wise words about love—romantic, brotherly, spiritual, and every kind of love in between—than almost anyone else in history. Prince, this book is dedicated 2 U.

# Contents

# Love, the Most F*cked Feeling of Them All

Much print has been dedicated to the subject of romantic relationships—why they're so hard to find, so difficult to maintain, so easily analogized to planets and pets—but the major source of trouble isn't that complicated. Too many people choose their partners based on excitement, lust, attraction, neediness . . . on *feelings*. Not surprisingly, as the authors of the book *F*ck Feelings*, we see that as a major problem.

While we've previously covered all manner of relationships, from voluntary (friendships, romantic partnerships) to involuntary (coworkers, neighbors, family, family, a thousand times family), this book is about searching for, maintaining, and surviving lasting romantic relationships.

Despite the (catchy, profane) title, *F*ck Love* isn't a manifesto that praises arranged marriages and claims that, due to her romcom filmography, Nancy Meyers is the Great Satan; it's a practical guide to finding someone whom you won't feel crazy about just until the honeymoon is over, in a partnership you can feel good about for life. This book teaches you how to do a pragmatic assessment of what *you're* into—or really what you need—so you don't obsess over whether he's *into you* and waste time on guys or gals who are easily described by airport bestsellers.

We don't tell you to reject love entirely, but to combine it with good management and a businesslike methodology. Put them together and you've got a fighting chance of either finding a good partner or at least not fucking up your life. This book might not help you find the person of your dreams, but it will provide you with the road map to avoiding the kind of nightmare relationships that probably caused you to buy books like this in the first place.

Before we can Sherpa you on your journey to the summit of Mt. Monogamy, however, let's break down exactly what we mean by a management/business approach, whom it's designed to guide, how it's best used, and, if used correctly, the kind of relationship you can expect to find at the end.

## Our Approach: See Yourself as a Romance Recruiter

Our term of choice for significant other—whether we're referring to a boyfriend, husband, old lady in a common-law relationship—is "partner," not just because it's a good catchall, but because we believe that strong partnership is at the core of any solid relationship. Our hearts, pop songs, and Oprahs may tell us that relationships exist to end loneliness or find eternal love, but our minds, bank accounts, and books we're reading at this second know that the real point of finding a mate is to have a good partner with whom you can build a good life.

That's why we encourage you to stop seeing your search as the quest for a soul mate or for marital contentment and start looking at yourself as a corporate headhunter out to find someone with whom you can run the business of life better than you can do it on your own.

That doesn't mean we think you should wind up with a partner you can work with but don't really like, or that love doesn't figure anywhere into the equation, and that discussions about who will take out the garbage will require you to write four TPS reports. Love and trust are important, but love doesn't last if your partner can't be relied on to do his portion of the work, make smart decisions, or keep promises, and if he doesn't share your long-term goals, whether they be having kids or training show ferrets.

The stakes for keeping a marriage and business afloat are both sky-high; if you can't work with your partner to survive financial problems, stagnancy, and the sometimes-crippling annoyance caused by the other guy's weaknesses and obnoxious habits, you risk the pain of bankruptcy, divorce, or personal ruin.

That's why investing in a long-term partnership/relationship is about the most dangerous thing you will ever do in your life—base jumping and relying on Boston's MBTA during a snowy winter included—and the business recruitment approach is the best way to screen out and avoid people who are bound to damage your life and break your heart, regardless of how desirable and exciting they seem in the short term.

So, you can love someone deeply, but if you can also work well together with that someone as a partner, you're much more apt to *like* each other after ten or twenty years. Which means, as hard as it may be for our romantically skewed minds to believe at first, the wish list of the human heart and of your average Head of Human Resources are remarkably similar.

This book isn't aimed just at people looking for a relationship, a.k.a. embarking on a hiring, but also at those who are having issues in relationships and marriages. Our approach works for anyone—married or single, gay or straight, dating around or considering settling down—who's looking for help finding, keeping, or improving a stable relationship.

Even if you're unsure about ever wanting a marriage or a lasting commitment, this book is still useful; good relationships are good relationships, whether they're romantic, close friendships, office based, or sex-centric temporary couplings. Knowing how to find good relationships in general and avoid the many, many ones that aren't is a skill you need to learn and practice all your life. Becoming relationship savvy isn't just necessary in order to find a relationship that lasts—especially since marriage isn't the right goal for everyone (see p. xxi)—but so you can protect yourself from unnecessary pain, complications, and legal action.

The most important thing you have to do in finding a good relationship is to screen out the bad ones that you're drawn to, so if you learn quickly from early heartbreaks and are naturally drawn to solid people, you don't need this book. If, however, like so many people, you find yourself drawn repeatedly into the same bad relationships, then our approach will help you figure out what you want that you just can't and shouldn't have and get more rational and methodical about screening.

No matter who you are or what kind of relationship you're in or seeking, success depends on your ability to recognize good character strengths when you see them, realize how vital they are to the long-term success of any relationship, and recruit them into your life.

## The Start of Your Search and
## the Basic Makeup of Our Map

Since you're going to be looking at your search or relationship through a business lens, begin by thinking seriously about your priorities and needs and, after considering what you can reasonably expect from a partner or prospect, put together a job description for your co-CEO of Marriage Inc. First, figure out the requirements of the job itself, from how much time you require (how many hours per week she'll have to put in), to what duties she'll be required to perform (from sharing in the pet-walking and dish-doing), to what special skills she'll need to possess (from spider-killing to baby-having).

Then, you need to determine what qualities a candidate should possess—the personal and character traits someone needs to qualify—and that's where this book first comes in.

Each chapter of this book is dedicated to exploring one of the most common traits that people claim to look for when searching for a partner: charisma, beauty, chemistry, communication, a sense of humor, a good family, intelligence, and wealth. Chapter by chapter, we break down how these traits can positively and negatively affect one's search, whether you're looking for that quality or living with it yourself. We also show how these traits contribute to a strong partnership by exploring their impact on three basic relationship stages—looking for people, dating them, and living with or marrying them.

Using examples inspired by the relationship problems that Dr. Bennett hears in his practice and/or that our readers submit to our advice blog, fxckfeelings.com, we show how each stage poses its own risks and rewards as you ask yourself, repeatedly, whether someone with a certain trait measures up to your requirements. If you decide a relationship is worthwhile despite unavoidable drawbacks, we also help you manage whatever is difficult and unlikely to change.

We identify red flags associated with each trait; this being a businesslike search, you have to do at least as much due diligence as your average HR department, minus the urine tests and with the possibility of eventually meeting the parents. Like any HR department, you must search efficiently or waste your resources, so you learn to drop candidates quickly once you know they aren't good enough.

Do your research by talking to his friends and relatives, not just about him as a person, but how he treated prior girlfriends (see table below for complete investigative techniques). Then immediately lose the résumé or phone number of a candidate if your research shows that his charisma often lets him get away with bad spending habits, or beauty blinds people to his brushes with the law; or he's a great communicator who often uses his skills to try to talk his way out of a problem with drugs or alcohol so severe that it can be perceived without a cup of pee.

At the end of each chapter, we identify five major elements that every solid relationship needs—mutual attraction, mutual respect, shared effort, common interests, and common goals—and describe the potentially positive and negative impact of that chapter's trait on each of those elements. That gives you a scorecard for rating these traits in candidates with the most potential.

We also provide you with a funny/serious lady-magazine-style quiz in each chapter, along with humorous sidebars that explain the art of apology (p. 100) and explore whether such romantic clichés as "the heart wants what it wants" (p. 196) or "there's someone for everyone" (p. 50) are "Truth, or Bullshit?" ("bullshit" and "bullshit unless you're totally unhygienic" respectively, which you'll just have to read to understand).

Once you've found likely candidates for an entry-level position, we recommend putting them through certain character-revealing tests to see if they're ready for management, such as helping you babysit your hell-spawn nephew or working with you to survive the aftermath of your shared experiment with gas-station sushi. Only then will you know whether you've met your goal and found someone who isn't just a good worker, but whom you work well with and, hopefully, you can get to take your business to the next level.

## Getting into the Basics of "Good Detective Work"

In this book we repeatedly advocate doing "good detective work," mostly when giving advice about how to determine whether a partner is reliable or a questionable behavior is likely to be habitual. While it may sound as if we're asking you to gather DNA samples or explain how time is a flat circle, we're actually just advising you to look at someone's history to determine whether he or she has a track record of bad behavior and its management.

That's because, if there's one thing that Dr. Bennett has learned from his many patients suffering in bad partnerships, it's that most relationships are what they are, most relationship problems arise from who people are, and most times they can't be fixed but could have been avoided if people had been more careful and thoughtful in the first place. Looking back at what is worst about a bad relationship, people almost always identify obvious red flags that should have warned them off but which they chose to ignore because they believed in the power of love (or therapy) to conquer all. Instead, therapy was merely conquering their deductible and their marriages were still doomed.

So, yes, some people can technically change, but so can a two-party political system, and if Dr. Bennett's experience or American history can teach us anything, it's that somebody who has a long history of cheating is as likely to stay faithful to you as is the United States to elect a Green Party president.

Here then are the behaviors that frequently deserve detective work, along with the places to do your investigation and the results to look for. None of this should involve excessive snooping or shady behavior because the kind of evidence you're looking for is rarely hidden: e.g., if you're worried that your special someone is bad with money, her creditors will make their presence and validation for your concern known.

Ultimately, all you're doing is a simple background check, because if somebody has a criminal relationship record, then you owe it to yourself to end things before the flat circle of romantic failures becomes truly infinite.

| Suspected Behavior | Where to Investigate | Hope to Find | Dread to Find |
|---|---|---|---|
| Infidelity | Facebook, but also through not-creepy conversations with her friends and family. If you're really suspicious, you can snoop around her cell phone, but if you cross the line from investigator to stalker, then you might want to cross the line from dating back to single. | No evidence or good reason to think she is, wants to, is likely to, etc., and that you were probably just being paranoid after she "forced you" to sit with her and watch all those Lifetime movies. | A YouTube clip of her being confronted by an ex on *Maury*, a dick pic gallery on her cell phone, friends and family whose stories could make up a multivolume oral history on cheating, etc. Upon being confronted, however, she insists she never meant it or will never do it again (while simultaneously being texted the image of a human penis). |

| Suspected Behavior | Where to Investigate | Hope to Find | Dread to Find |
|---|---|---|---|
| Flakiness | Start with your own calendar to see which events he was late for or forgot entirely, then compare notes with his nearest and dearest. Maybe give him small tests of reliability—assignments to pick up a shirt at the dry cleaner or make dinner plans with friends—and see if he follows through or holds a steady flaking pattern. | He's normally reliable but going through a rough patch due to a transition at work or a noisy upstairs neighbor or daylight saving time. Or, if he does have a tendency to flake, he's aware of it, not defensive about it, and has learned some tricks to help him remember to get the most important stuff done on time. | He insists he's got it together, but it's the credit-card or cable or power companies that lose his payments, although the debt collectors obviously don't want to hear the truth. It's also not his fault that he hasn't kept a job longer than six months, and he wasn't lying when he told you he got that thing done, even though he hasn't and never will. |
| Inability to say no or to prioritize requests | Check out his schedule, tracking how he spends his time and money, because if he's giving whole evenings to his needy and awful aunt while you only got to see him for a ten-minute lunch break that week, then you're seeing solid evidence of poor prioritizing. | After you ask him, without anger, to consider a better approach to time management, he's able to see the benefits to sometimes saying no and finds his own good reasons for saying no to unreasonable demands. | He treats your concerns as if you're unreasonably needy (unlike his wretched aunt who needs him to come over and inventory her sports bras) and insensitive to his needs. Of course, when you tell him you want to break up, you become the squeakiest wheel, so he gives you the most attention . . . until the crisis abates. |

# F*ck Love

| Suspected Behavior | Where to Investigate | Hope to Find | Dread to Find |
|---|---|---|---|
| Financial irresponsibility | Any available financial documents, or just look casually at her mail for anything marked "Final Notice." Ask about whether she keeps a budget or has a rainy-day fund or even an old jar filled with loose change and extra shirt buttons. | She admits to having accrued some debt but has since learned to monitor her spending and is working on making herself a reasonable budget, even if sticking to it during sample-sale season is often hopeless. | She says she has it totally under control since she pays out maxed cards by signing up for new cards and maxing *them* out, and also, whenever she gets too deep in the hole, she just emails this guy in Russia for a new identity (although she won't tell you her real name until you've been together for six months) (and you've lent her $5,000). |
| Drug or alcohol abuse | His behavior; e.g., changes in the way he acts, talks, and smells. Keep an eye out for mystery expenses, shady excuses, and, if you're really hungry for proof, empty bottles or full baggies squirreled away in his home. | He's got an actual medical condition that explains what you've noticed, such as a neurological condition or low blood sugar. Or he's got a bona fide addiction, but he's aware that it's a problem and you've got good reason to believe he's committed to, and starting to benefit from, treatment. | Addiction, lies, and pleas for understanding and forgiveness, especially for all that money he stole from you and for giving you HPV that he must've gotten from a fellow crack enthusiast. |

| Suspected Behavior | Where to Investigate | Hope to Find | Dread to Find |
|---|---|---|---|
| Other asshole behavior | In restaurants, specifically, how he treats waitstaff, bartenders, or anyone in the service industry. Always goes after what he wants, whether or not it's good for him, you, or anyone else. | Knows he can be a jerk, especially when he's tired and the cuisine is vegetarian. Ultimately, however, he doesn't just apologize but actually tries to do better. | Blames the waiter for being slow, you for making an issue of it and not taking his side, and the Lord for making him the last righteous man in a world gone mad (aside from his actual lord and savior, Donald Trump). |

## Where or to Whom Our Map Leads

Even if we thought it was worth searching for a partner based on how many butterflies he filled your stomach with—a change of heart that could only be caused for us by a major stroke—we all know that the butterfly stage of relationships doesn't, and can't, last. Anybody who can stay utterly giddy about any one thing over several decades is either a goldfish or has had several strokes himself.

It's not that love and romance aren't supposed to be an important, enjoyable part of the search, but since neither is that important in the day-to-day function of a successful marriage, and since we believe that defective partnership, not failed romance, is the chief cause of divorce, the relationship this book should help you find will be more about reliability than romance, more about trust than lust.

Our approach is meant to help you find someone you may not be romantically interested in one day—because her personality could be flattened by a severe depression, or his beauty may be damaged by age or illness, or a flood or bankruptcy or responsibility for a demented parent hasn't just drained the joy from your life but the

blood from your genitals—but with whom, even after being hit with
a shitload of bad luck, you share an interest in each other's company,
an unbreakable trust, and many good laughs about every shitty
thing you've been through. A strong partnership isn't about eternal
love but an external support system with which you can survive all
manner of bullshit.

When decent people with compatible values spend a life together
and build something that is good and greater than themselves, they
usually wind up loving one another deeply and enhancing each
other's sense of safety, contentment, and trust. It doesn't sound as
sexy as the promise of fairy-tale romance, but if there's anything
less sexy than a successful long-term relationship—in which both
parties have washed each other's dirty underwear, cleaned up baby
puke, and seen more galling tantrums than they'd want to count—
we're not sure what it is.

If you're unsure if marriage is the right goal for you or are even
panicking because you worry it will never happen, it's important to
remember that it's okay to remain unhitched and that living with
the wrong spouse is much worse than living alone with just the right
number of friends to have your back. Everybody has her own needs,
tastes, and standards, and it's important to determine accordingly
what's best for you, regardless of what cultural stigma, family pressure, or your wish to get a set of fancy plates without paying for it
are telling you about what the best choice is, period.

Think hard about your criteria for what you want in a partner
or friend and stick to those criteria no matter how long, lonely, and
infuriating the search can be. If marriage is what you want, particularly as a way to start a family, then your criteria must be more selective and exacting, but your expectations must remain reasonable,
since all you can do is conduct a good search and make the best of

your luck. Letting neediness or an overdetermination to get married force you into relationships that don't meet your basic standards is a good way to ruin your life.

Don't feel obliged to know whether you want to pursue marriage. Yes, it's important to think hard about whether marriage is the right goal for you, but it's also important to realize that you can't predict what your needs, romantic opportunities, or general mind-set might be in the future.

Don't begin your search by deciding resolutely that marriage is either right for you or something you'd die to avoid. Instead, learn what's important to you, not just in a partner, but in your own future, regardless of the pressures that come from your friends, family, and the white-dress industry. Even if you believe marriage isn't for you, you should always leave yourself open to the possibility of a plan B while knowing that you're perfectly happy with your plan A (lone).

Most important, whether or not you end up getting hitched, remember that the only person you're obliged to spend your entire life with is you, so if one of the major motivations for finding someone is so you can be with yourself less, then you need to adjust your mind-set. You don't need to love yourself to love somebody else (please forgive us, Lord Ru), but you do need to want a partnership that is beneficial to each other's growth and character, not just a self-serving distraction from your loneliness and self-loathing. Essentially, the best reason to invest in any relationship is because you believe it will make *both* your lives better; if it doesn't, then you're better off being alone.

## Do You Have the Marriage Mind-Set?

A lot of factors go into deciding whether to commit to someone that have nothing to do with how much two people love each other or how much he spent on a clear pebble. Here are some of those factors that determine whether marriage is a smart goal and high priority, not really necessary, or the object of so many intense needs that it should be reconsidered after breathing into a bag and thinking about the future, not through a cloud of fear.

| | Ready to Make Marriage a Top Priority | Comfortable with Marriage as a Medium Priority | Prioritizing Marriage Panic over Rational Thought |
|---|---|---|---|
| Kids | You want kids, but know you don't have the temperament, finances, or family support to do it on your own, so partnership is a necessary beginning if you want a family. | You're unsure about wanting kids, but are willing to do the preparation (saving money, freezing eggs, soliciting willing gays) to have one of your own one day if you decide you need a kid in your life. | You're not sure you want kids, but are just terrified of missing the boat and filling your bottomless regret with cats, bitterness, and a long, lonely, cliché-filled march to the grave. |

|  | Ready to Make Marriage a Top Priority | Comfortable with Marriage as a Medium Priority | Prioritizing Marriage Panic over Rational Thought |
|---|---|---|---|
| Money | Even by working hard and developing your skills, you don't have enough money for the lifestyle and security you think are important. You're independent, but partnership would make a big difference. | You have enough money to support yourself and are comfortable living a modest lifestyle, which is the most prudent way to live on your salary, since you value your independence. | You think you make enough money, but looking at your bank statements gives you hives and makes you long for a spouse who could just take care of you. |
| Companionship | You've never liked being alone, but you've learned to do it well as a way of avoiding dangerous compromises with partners from hell. You'll be happy when you can hang out with a steady roommate and worry less about your social calendar. | You enjoy the company of friends, but like periods of quiet solitude even more and are perfectly happy to spend time alone, watching TV in your apartment, reading in a bar, or carving chain-saw sculptures in a remote cabin. | You're convinced you may be the world's first FOMO fatality; you hate the feeling of being alone, being left out, and generally missing out on the kind of fun you have with others (which is the only kind of fun). |

# F*ck Love

|  | Ready to Make Marriage a Top Priority | Comfortable with Marriage as a Medium Priority | Prioritizing Marriage Panic over Rational Thought |
|---|---|---|---|
| Sex | You're finished with experiments, conquests, and enforced celibacy and appreciate comfort, familiarity, reliability, and wanting to be together regardless. | For any variety of reasons—a less active libido, or the ability to store up the benefits of intimacy gathered from random hookups like a sex camel—you're comfortable not having sex frequently, consistently, or not anonymously. | You need to lock someone down now so you won't have to worry about the years when you're so fat, old, and bald or as hairy as a Market Street bear that your genitals will fall off from disuse. Plus, the second you're hitched, you can relax and start eating bread again. |
| Support | You know your weak spots and could use a trusted adviser/supervisor/ friend to remind you that you're not so bad when the negative thoughts start to seem real. | You don't need a lot of reassurance to make decisions or deal with everyday hassles; if anything, you prefer to decompress and think through problems by yourself. | You fall apart without your friends, but your friends are all pairing off and getting married, and you do not want to be the cheese that stands alone (or even eat cheese; see above). |

\* \* \*

So for now, whether or not you've got marriage in mind, use the advice in this book to find just the kind of person you need, and forget those dates who fall short, taking it day by day, dinner by dinner, and, alas, jerk by jerk. If you're on board with this book's businesslike approach, it's time to get down to business and approach your search. Be smart, make thoughtful decisions, and don't let any emotion, be it love or fear, have too much influence over your quest for better relationships, a possible partner, and a plan for your future.

# F*ck
# Love

# Chapter 1

# F*ck Charisma

Unlike other attractive superficial qualities—looks, finances, a handbag so exclusive it has a first name—charisma can't be faked or procured. As appealing traits go, it's a double whammy because it's not just inherently ingratiating, but, like blond hair or a high metabolism, it's a genetic gift; true charismatics are born, not made, and they possess the kind of magnetic charm that makes everybody like them and want to believe everything they say, no matter how high the bullshit quotient. That a charismatic person makes us feel good on so many levels, however, is a sign that he's not necessarily good to build a life with.

Charisma is even more effective than other superficial qualities at drawing you to people who, were they slightly less charming, you'd quickly realize were human plague. Charisma can blind you to character traits you need to be looking at and compromise your future, safety, and common sense. On the other hand, being attracted to someone who's totally uncharismatic is about as likely as having a crush on a floor lamp.

You're most susceptible to charismatic relationships if you feel bored with life and unhappy with yourself, e.g., when you're broke and lonely, unhappy at work, or generally feeling useless, unattractive, and miserable. That's when contact with charisma promises to lift you out of the doldrums and imbue your life with excitement that would otherwise never happen.

Unfortunately, most of us are unhappy or bored at some time in our lives. What makes us particularly vulnerable to the seduction of charisma is the feeling that, just because we can't make our lives better and more interesting, we're failures. That's when secondhand charisma feels like a magic power that can transform us from losers to winners, from unlovable to the most beloved, special creatures in the world.

Ironically, thinking your charisma makes you special is just as dangerous. You'd think you'd love your charismatic self and its ability to get dates, above-your-true-ability job opportunities, and every last call returned. After the excitement passes, however, you're left with a job or relationship that, for various reasons, may not work and is often boring. Since you need to generate excitement to feel like a success, you always have to move on, often leaving in your wake a lot of people who feel angry and betrayed.

Charisma is inherently magnetic, but just when it seems to draw you into a deeper connection, it's most likely to pull you under, blinding you to what's going to happen next or addicting you to searches that lead nowhere.

## The Good Things You Want Charisma to Deliver

- A feeling of significance in everything you're saying and doing with this magical significant someone.
- A sense of confidence that allows you to approach people so easily you're basically "the human whisperer."
- A glow from feeling that a fascinating person finds you fascinating and everyone else in the room is total bullshit.
- A relief from the way you hated yourself and your life before this person made you and your life seem downright lovable.
- A confidence that comes from knowing you're with the right person, in the right place, and all is right with the world.

## Profile of the Charismatic

Traits associated with people seen as charismatics include:

- *Physical attributes:* Expert at knowing just how to approach you, smile at you, lock eyes with you, and "accidentally" touch you to convey confidence and connection, regardless of how they actually feel about themselves, you, or anything else.
- *Common occupations:* Those that turn connection and respect into money, such as preaching, litigating, politicking, acting, and big-ticket selling (mansions, boats, huge yachts that are actually mansion-boats, etc.).
- *What attracts you first:* Some intangible quality that commands your attention for reasons that aren't clear, i.e., isn't based on attractiveness, intelligence, or anything short of hypnotism.
- *Other early red flags:* Your inability to put your finger on what you like about him, aside from his ability to make a strong

impression; basically, in describing this person, you sound as if you're talking about a delightful new street drug instead of a human, and other people in his orbit seem to agree.

### Seeking Charisma

Charisma seems like an ideal quality for drawing people together since it inspires attraction and respect and has more to do with personality than beauty or wealth. It protects one from the pain of rejection and the embarrassment of bombing at dinner parties. While charisma might be less superficial than some traits, it still exists fairly close to the surface; charisma has nothing to do with character, reliability, or impulse management, and it's less than ideal for predicting reliability, fidelity, and a capacity for hard work. Being charmed can give you fuzzy feelings for someone; it can also give you the wrong idea about the person you think you should be with.

Here are three examples:

- *I have a friend at work who's got a magnetic personality and I enjoy talking to her, but I never know whether she really likes me or is just being her usual attractive self. I always get the feeling when we're talking that I'm special to her, but she sounds like that with other people, too, and I don't want to make a move at work that could then make things embarrassing. My goal is to figure out whether her feelings for me are special, or whether she's naturally magnetic and I'm just part of her entourage.*

- *My boyfriend is tremendously attractive, and I know he loves me, but he also loves attention, and I think he has trouble saying no to at least some of his many female fans. He's a great salesman, which means he's such a great bullshitter that he's good at bull-*

*shitting himself. My goal is to figure out whether he's capable of a committed relationship.*

- *People love my girlfriend because she's totally spontaneous and fun to be with, but I see the other side, which is that she's also sometimes angry and mistrustful, and that's when I wonder what our relationship would be like if we got serious. My goal is to help her get over her insecurities, so she can be the happy, charming person we all love.*

Charisma seems like a desirable asset in a long-term relationship because it doesn't wear out or depend on looks or money; after all, 'tis nobler to choose someone with a good personality over good cheekbones or a good investment portfolio. Unfortunately, having a good personality and just being good at attracting people are rarely the same thing.

One problem with seeking a relationship with a charismatic person is that it's often hard to tell whether she likes you as much as she seems to and, at the crush stage, whether your first overtures will be accepted or rejected. The real issue, however, is not whether you may suffer a little humiliation when you discover that the intense interest, intimate conversation, and love-song-strength eye contact don't really reflect more than your crush's desire to captivate. It's that, even if she is interested, she may never belong to you as much as she belongs to her public.

So instead of trying to figure out whether this woman is actually interested in you or is this way with everyone, take a moment to determine whether she's actually worth pursuing in the first place, since a relationship with her is bound to make you feel neglected, insecure, and possibly angry and jealous. You may find that it would be better to keep her as a friend you can harmlessly flirt with while looking for someone else more meaningful, even if that someone is less magnetic.

Indeed, a charismatic partner may always make you feel unsure about how much she actually cares, so once you notice her using her charm on anyone or anything that's currently holding her attention, you start to wonder who's most-est special to her, or whether anyone is. You're right, then, to put on the brakes until you can watch her behavior, gather information about her past relationships, and verify her ability to treat those who are truly close, such as you, with genuine specialness and in a way that lasts.

If you're dating someone who depends on charisma to feel good, as well as to make a living, as do many salespeople, you have additional reason to worry. His manager, ego, and income tell him that he's respected for his excellent ability to seduce new sales. Unless he is grounded in better values, however, and can tolerate the inevitable "chopped liver" feeling that burdens even the best of partnerships, your relationship may not endure. At the least, those eventual feelings of neglect may fuel a strong need to seek admiration and conquest (those usually come by not being sexually neglected by someone else).

Before taking a risk and putting yourself on the line to commit to that charismatic person, find out all you can about past and current relationships. Instead of just paying attention to his enthusiasm and generosity when love is new, ask yourself whether his attachments last after things get unpleasant and annoying, i.e., after an episode of food poisoning or Thanksgiving dinner with your alcoholic grandfather. Get to know his values and observe how much he depends on his charisma to feel good.

Charisma can also disguise the usual high-risk personality traits that make lasting relationships difficult. If someone with a great, relaxed public persona turns out to have a bad temper and little trust in private, don't assume that your love and attention will restore the personal warmth that always seemed to dominate her personality before you got close.

While bursts of anger and mistrust may be rooted in misunderstanding or temporary depression and may resolve with patience and understanding, don't let wishful thinking cloud your judgment as you get to know someone and learn about what happened to their prior relationships. Charismatic people often have more control over how they present themselves; prepare to take more time, effort, and detective work to know who they really are by observing their deeds, rather than responding to their charm.

Charisma may grab your interest and make someone seem like a safe bet, but as with any deal that seems too good to be true, it probably is. The more charisma attracts you, the more carefully you should examine that person's character and his ability to stand by values of partnership and faithfulness, even when he's tempted by offers of admiration, money, and sex that his charisma can snag for him as easily as it hooked you.

### Quiz: Charm Questions — Caught by Charisma

1. If the most popular kid in your class or guy in your office or gentleman on your floor of the assisted-living facility sidled up to you and asked you out on a date, you would:

   A: Say yes before the offer is withdrawn or he even finishes asking the question.

   B: Say no with conviction, to make it clear you haven't forgotten the years of rejection and indifference you've been subjected to by him and all of his kind.

   C: Buy time by chatting about what he thinks would be fun to do on this hypothetical date while you try to figure out how full of shit he might be and what's really going on.

2.  If you spot your favorite professional hockey player at the super-
    market, ask him for a selfie, and he starts to get chummy after-
    ward, your instinct would be to:
    A:  Gush about how you are a big fan and loved when he punched
        that guy from his rival team so hard he got concussed.
    B:  Let him know you're a fan, not a whore, and you appreciate
        his time but your Lean Cuisines are melting and it's time to
        go.
    C:  Take his number but avoid using it until after Google assures
        you that he's not married, a moron, or out on bail for using
        his punching abilities on his last girlfriend.

3.  If the young upstart candidate running for Congress crosses the
    street to shake your hand, smile at you, and ask for your vote,
    your reaction would be to:
    A:  Try to impress her with jokes, maybe get a big hug, and blush
        as she puts one of her campaign pins on your coat.
    B:  Run the other way while yelling, "Leave me alone! I'm . . . an
        anarchist! Fuck the system!"
    C:  Smile, tell her you'll think about it and appreciate her atten-
        tion, and wish her luck.

4.  You hated high school with the passionate intensity of a suicide
    bomber, but if the coolest kid from your class—the one every-
    one wanted and who didn't know you existed—called you as an
    alumni rep to raise money for your alma mater, you would:
    A:  Tell him you'd be honored to give and happily follow his lead
        into a conversation filled with loving nostalgia for a place you
        neither loved nor feel nostalgic for.
    B:  Let him know if he'd actually known you, he would know that
        you hated school and would never have bothered calling in

the first place, so it's time to move on to the next sucker on the list.

C: If the gift would help outsider students like you to enjoy the school more, give a prudent amount, but otherwise, politely decline.

5. If your glamorous mother-in-law takes you and your husband out for a fancy dinner where she pitches you both on investing another $1,000 in her business, you tell her:

A: That you'd be happy to help, expecting your generosity will strengthen your relationship with this impossibly chic woman and give you entrée into her exciting world.

B: That she's forgetting all the money she already owes you and your husband, which she could have paid off if she'd spent less money on impressing and charming people with pointy shoes and fancy meals.

C: That you'd love to help, but you'd need to see a loose budget from her first, just to see if the money would be used wisely, then take a look at your own household budget to see what you can afford.

6. When your spouse gets through her contrite explanation for why she has been so busy with social engagements that you haven't had a chance to talk in a week, you respond:

A: That you totally understand and are just proud to be associated with someone who's so admired, well connected, and hardworking.

B: Flatly tell her that it's fine while mentally plotting how you're going to find a private detective to tail your spouse after you stay up scouring her cell-phone records.

C: That you both need to sit down and determine the amount of time together that you believe the relationship needs and see whether agreement is possible.

If you answered mostly A's . . .

You need to take time to develop your bullshit meter because right now you're far too easily swept away by the often-false flattery, meaning, and devotion that charismatic people are so good at delivering. You don't want to let facts spoil the warm fuzzies, but you need to learn how to pursue them if you want to protect yourself from exploitation, doom, and other bullshit you don't even want to imagine.

If you answered mostly B's . . .

Then you have a charisma allergy; if you so much as breathe in a particle of the stuff, it hits hard, stirring up uncomfortable fear and envy, feeling like a personal attack that will end in your deception and humiliation unless you strike back. Unfortunately, you may be attacking a nice, honest person who can't help being charismatic but is otherwise worth getting to know, so build up a little resistance so you can encounter charisma without immediate negative side effects.

If you answered mostly C's . . .

You're at peace with the charismatics you encounter in your life, able to enjoy the pleasure of their enchanting company and tolerate its uncertainties without forgetting yourself or the life lessons you've learned about character and lasting relationships. As long as you keep going slow, ignore the rush, and pay attention to what's actually happening when things are not so much fun, you'll be able to peacefully coexist with charming types without being too charmed yourself.

## Where's Your Partner on the Charisma Scale?

We wouldn't be with our partners if we didn't find something attractive in their personalities, but while some spouses' appeal is due to a subtle, earnest nature, others are so enchanting that their magnetism isn't just undeniable, it's dangerous. Your average spouse can find a way to talk you into doing something you dislike by working out a compromise, but a not-charming partner can be so genuinely obnoxious that he works your last nerve, and a too-smooth spouse is actually working you all the time like a mark. Here are a few common relationship scenarios that highlight the risks and the benefits of having a partner who's either as charismatic as a paper clip, has average appeal, or could charm the pants off a statue.

| Charisma Impaired | Charisma Capable | Charisma Corrupted |
|---|---|---|
| Keeps mentioning that *somebody* needs to do the dishes, observing how dirty the dishes are, recalling that he had such a lovely dream about pristine mugs and plates and an empty sink, and is generally as convincing and passive-aggressive as a sweaty used-car salesman. | Gives you a dirty look every time you pass the kitchen without going in, but after so many arguments, finds the money to buy you a dishwasher that's so tech'd out and fancy it makes you want to wash dishes that are clean just so you can play with your new kitchen toy. | If attempts to flirt you into dish-doing have failed, he plans more dinners with old frat buddies, guys from the club, and women he insists are clients, so you wind up begging to cook for him *and* do dishes since you feel as if he were doing you a favor just by eating with you at home. |

| Charisma Impaired | Charisma Capable | Charisma Corrupted |
| --- | --- | --- |
| Goes hog wild on Sephora's website and successfully hides the cosmetic arsenal until the credit-card bill arrives, at which point she terrifies you with projectile lip gloss and elbow cream until you agree she can keep everything. | Overdoes Sephora but agrees to cut back in other ways and return that sparkly lip stuff that looks ridiculous anyway . . . if you put away the refund so you can eventually make good on your promise to buy yourself a suit that fits. | Makes you forget how much cash she burned through by putting on a face so fabulous that she makes you feel as if you were on the arm of a movie star, even if you're going to the nearby Panera Bread instead of the Golden Globes. |
| Flirts and texts clumsily with someone he met at a bar, then, after you find out when he forgets his phone at home, he becomes too afraid to come home and face you, and you start to wonder if you care. | Gives a sloppy, cringe-worthy drunk performance at your office Christmas party that causes many not-merry fights, but starts the New Year with a determination to get sober that restores your faith, at least temporarily. | You find a strange text on his phone, but he insists it's the crazy lady at work who's always flirting with him but he only has eyes for you, because you're so gorgeous and make up his whole world (cue intense eye contact, drop phone). |

## Having Charisma

To the uncharismatic—those who were never brushed with the pixie dust of charm and have to rely on luck, extra hard work, and the ability to beat back nagging self-doubt to achieve any kind of success—having charisma can seem like the ultimate advantage. A charismatic person appears to have access to a better, luckier kind of luck than the rest of us. Unfortunately, as we've seen with too many lottery winners, freak survivors of catastrophes, and celebrity spawn, too much luck can be a bad thing, and too much of this kind of luck can also ruin your life if you don't understand its costs and risks and manage them carefully.

Here are three examples:

- *My buddies envy me because girls always want to be with me. It should be good for my ego, but I don't feel comfortable just using girls for sex and have trouble saying no because I hate to make anyone feel rejected. So after we have a date or two, they wind up getting really invested, and since I rarely am, I wind up having to let them down after they've started to care. I feel terribly guilty and worn-out by the whole process, but I'm not sure what the alternative is—whether it's up-front or after a few dates, I'm going to end up making these girls feel like shit. My goal is to figure out a way to turn off my charisma so I don't have to reject girls all the time.*

- *I've always felt lucky to be someone who's good at making friends and getting along with people in general. I'm even friends with all of my exes, since they're all nice guys worth keeping in my life. Now, however, I find myself fascinated with a guy who's really smart with a wicked sense of humor, but also prickly and a bit of a loner. I thought I'd have an easy time getting past his defenses, but the closer we get, the more I get to see his irritable, nasty side. My goal is to figure out how to help this guy, whom I really like, to become more relaxed with people in general and me in particular.*

- *I love dating and am blessed with the mysterious ability to attract whatever guys I want. But then, after a couple months, what starts out as genuine interest always seems to fade on my side, but not on theirs. I don't know what's wrong with me. I love the initial*

*attention, but it's not like I'm desperate for it and willing to get*
*it from anyone; I'm pretty choosy in terms of only getting into*
*relationships with guys I really like who meet my high standards.*
*My goal is to understand why I get bored with really great guys.*

Having charisma is like belonging to an elite club with many privileges and benefits; it's the Amex Black Card of personality traits, giving one boundless access to everything from business contacts to dates to private jets (why not?). Whether it's your charm or your credit that's unlimited, however, there's always a danger of forgetting what all that privilege and access will end up costing you in the end.

Charisma often misleads people into thinking that they have more control over relationships than they do, distracts them from examining character factors that determine whether a relationship is safe or dangerous, and burdens them with an unreasonable sense of responsibility for the feelings of others. So if you don't keep those risks in mind, you may end up going into emotional debt.

When charisma makes you lucky at romance, and you're lucky enough to have the good character to recognize and respect your gift, it's hard not to feel guilty. After all, you're receiving attention that others must work much harder to achieve and which you don't deserve for any reason other than that you're charmed and charming. Unless you're in love with your charisma, you may well feel an obligation to offer something in return for this attention, such as not disappointing all those people who are unlucky enough to be drawn to your gift/curse.

Unfortunately, making yourself available to admirers can't create a real, lasting relationship and will make their disappointment worse when you stop answering their calls or acting like a real friend. Feeling guilty can cause harm and make you feel guiltier.

Instead of making yourself responsible for meeting their needs, remember that your goal isn't to give every charmed party a chance, but to find a lasting relationship despite the often-confusing and time-consuming overresponsiveness of possible candidates, and to do so while causing as little harm as possible. So, without being rude or obnoxious, learn to turn off your charm, turn down the smile, and stick to topics that are neutral and a little boring, at least until you decide whether you like someone. Don't stop trying to get to know prospective dates, but don't be afraid to use clichés and make a dull first impression. That way, when you seem to express interest, it will be because your interest is real and you're ready for a real response.

People who have the charisma to build close friendships with little effort often find it hard to understand loners and others who find friendship difficult. Charismatics come to feel that there isn't a person in the world whom they can't turn into a friend if they want to, so socially inhibited people and grumps become a thrilling challenge.

Unfortunately, while it's easy for a charismatic person to warm up the shy and awkward, no one can make relationships turn out well with an Asshole, and the effort to create a positive relationship with such a person is bound to end badly. That's because Assholes can't stop themselves from turning on their friends, and they make no exception for warm, friendly people with charisma. On the contrary, the warmer the relationship at the beginning, the hotter the explosion when it disappoints.

So don't assume that charisma and a gift for friendship can overcome all obstacles and are under your complete control. Your goal isn't to make friends with all those who interest you, but to instead take the same self-protective precautions as are necessary for everyone else. If you tried to tame a beast, give yourself credit for courage and altruism, but if the beast turns out to be too feral, return it to the cave where you found it, give yourself credit for learning an important, if painful, lesson, and warn your fellow hikers to give it a wide berth.

If you're truly particular when it comes to partners, having charisma creates additional problems because now you're dealing with a second uncontrollable factor, which is pickiness. Truly picky people don't just have high standards, they are rarely comfortable with friends who aren't a particularly good match. Charisma and a genuine interest in getting to know people may propel you into many relationships that initially gather speed, but then pickiness may kill the engine and leave your relationship in a ditch.

Yes, it's possible you're afraid of commitment or are too much in love with flirting to move on to the stress of everyday partnership. In those cases, talking over your issues with a therapist may make a difference. What's also possible, however, is that your gift for dating is combined with an innate selectiveness that can't easily be overridden.

Just because you're great with relationships, find dating a breeze, and go out with genuinely nice, interesting people doesn't mean that you can talk yourself out of pickiness. So, instead of letting hot dates turn into serial disappointments, develop other ways of socializing and amusing yourself while getting to know prospective dates more gradually. Don't cross the dating line until you think someone may actually meet your picky standards. Then, even if things don't work out, you'll know you avoided causing unnecessary pain.

Yes, having charisma confers luck and gives you choices you might not otherwise have. It does not, however, give you control over the qualities that make a relationship last, and it often makes things look good when they aren't. Charisma can make it easy to pair off with anyone, but it's up to you to figure out what you need from someone and learn to say no to everyone else.

**Classic Lack-of-Charisma Remedies for Those Seeking Women**

Things you can do if you can't woo ladies with natural charm:

- Learn to play a stringed instrument, such as a guitar or a bass. Avoid instruments you can't lift (harp) or play without sweating profusely (drums) or simply hold without looking like a moron (tuba).
- Don't ever leave the house in sweatpants, pajamas, shower shoes, or any clothes that strengthen the impression you've just awoken from a coma.
- Consult the necessary sources—hip publications, an ex you're still friendly with, your gayest gay friend—to get a decent, maintenance-minimal, cost-more-than-$10 haircut.
- If you know you can handle it, adopt a dog. Not only will it attract the opposite sex, it will weed out unworthy mates who can't handle hair, drool, or crypt breath.
- At the very least, don't publicly scratch, clip, pluck, pick, or drain almost any part of your body, certainly not those parts normally covered by clothing.

## Marriage and Charisma

Charisma may always be attractive to some people, and some people may always be charismatic, but nobody always lies within the Venn diagram between the two; no one's guaranteed to be held in the thrall of one person's charisma forever. That's why, if charm is the main force driving your marriage, sooner or later you're in trouble. Charisma doesn't *have* to screw up a marriage, but it comes with unique baggage, and it's your job to know what trouble to look for and what to screen out.

Here are three examples:

- *Before I met my wife, when we were in medical school, it was no secret that she was the most fascinating person on campus.*

*Professors treated her like an equal and were eager to mentor her for valuable internships, and everyone wanted to be her friend. So when she found me interesting, I couldn't believe it. My problem is that, even though we've been married ten years, she still hungers for admirers. She loves me and our children and is a good, hardworking person, but she can't leave a room until everyone has been charmed, and it often means that our family comes last. Sometimes I think she gets flirtatious and it goes too far. My goal is to get her to draw the line before she has an affair and blows our partnership apart.*

- *I don't mind that my wife is shy and not terribly sociable; I've always been a big socializer and popular, and I guess opposites attract. My schmoozing skills have taken me far in my profession, but now I've reached the stage in my career where it helps if she comes with me to these parties to show that I'm grounded, and she just hates it. She says it's all phony and a waste of time. My goal is to figure out how to put her at ease so she can do the social scene and I can succeed at the next stage of my career.*

- *My father is one of the most interesting people I ever met—everyone finds him fascinating—but by the time I was ten, I realized he was a con man. He didn't mean to hurt people, but he considered it part of his job to raise money for projects and investments, and when they didn't work out, he'd just disappear. He'd either move the family or, after my mother divorced him, he'd reappear after the heat blew over. I am angry at him and can't trust him, but I also love him, and now I just wish he could get help. My goal is to convince him to get help or, at least, to forgive him for all the harm he did our family and a lot of other people as well.*

A common fear among the mostly young and commitment-adverse is that, after many years of marriage, they will get bored with whomever they've saddled themselves. They will fall out of love and end up finding someone new, then finding a lawyer, then finding themselves single and living in their car, giving their ex every cent they make. They will be doomed to die alone (see the sidebar on p. 22).

A charismatic partner seems like the solution to that problem; if you can find someone who's inherently fascinating, the excitement will never end. What you don't realize, however, is that the fascination begins to fail when someone doesn't keep his promises, clean up after himself, or generally hold up his end of the marriage bargain. In addition, the spark that compulsive fascinators rely on to attract others either starts a fire or flames out; it seems as if the spark will burn forever, but once he has you fired up, he has to keep finding something new to ignite.

Charisma can be as addictive to those who have it as it is to those who are attracted to it, becoming so essential to achieving one's ambitions that it becomes okay to subvert the values of honesty, fidelity, and hard work. Understanding its influence and possible long-term problems can help you avoid those issues or, if you didn't see them coming, help you to respond with less blame and more effectiveness.

If your fascinating partner is a compulsive fascinator, it doesn't necessarily mean that she loves you less or is less committed to your family. It may just mean that, like JFK, FDR, or W"B"JC (husband of HRM HRC), she gets such a charge out of winning people over that she can't stop herself from taking that extra step and sometimes sexualizing her connections. That her sparkage often advances her career, however, and indirectly benefits your life together makes it even harder for her to stop, and you can't help feeling hurt.

Remember, however, that your partnership may still provide commitment, economic security, and good parenting, and breaking it up may be worse than keeping it together. HRC is no fool, even if she chose to suffer one.

Before deciding what to do, measure the depth of your partner's other attachments compared to hers with you. Focus on actions, not words, as you examine her response to your and the children's needs and her ability to make a positive difference in your life. Look at time invested, money spent, and difficulties endured. You may decide that infidelity of any kind, even if it's not physical, is unacceptable. But you may discover that her other love is merely an addiction to the buzz of reflected charisma and, for all the damage done, is an insignificant distraction that presents little threat to the specialness of your partnership.

If, before deciding whether to move on, you wish to test the ability of a charismatic partner to limit seductive behavior, approach the problem as you would any addiction. Spell out the behavior that you find unacceptable, and urge her to regard it as destructive to her goals and values. Don't ask her to change for your sake; ask whether she thinks she needs to change for herself. Then observe the actions she takes and whether, like attending 12-step meetings, they reflect a new and continued commitment to sexual abstinence with anyone but you.

If you're the one with charisma to burn and your partner is relatively antisocial, it's natural to want to share your good times with your partner and to resent her inability to appreciate or support your social accomplishments. You may well feel closer, at times, to those who are more like yourself and have more respect for your public persona.

Remember, however, that charisma may often distract you from important, unglamorous priorities, such as caring for kids and doing your share of domestic dirty work, and that your partner's perspective may help balance your life, even as it deflates your ego and kills your party buzz. Instead of valuing your partnership by how well it contributes to social success, list your other priorities and imagine yourself single.

Create a job/spouse description that covers your most important obligations as well as the things you enjoy doing. Then determine your partner's contributions and ask yourself whether she does jobs that you don't like doing and allows you to do what you're good at.

Yes, you need a partner who accepts your charisma-driven socializing, but you may also benefit from her efforts to limit your social activities, pull you away, and engage you in other obligations. Don't overreact to her criticism and disrespect until you first look at her overall influence on the life you want to lead.

Perhaps the worst-case scenario, when you love a charismatic person, is to discover he's a coldhearted manipulator whose need to attract and influence people far exceeds his honesty or ability to keep a commitment. He feels good only when he's charming people (which he can do without effort) and can't stand it when he's not. He compulsively feeds you what you want to hear and can't tell the truth if he knows it will upset you or even when it doesn't matter, because it's a habit he can't break.

Like the compulsive seducer, the con man is addicted to his own charisma, but unlike a decent person who sometimes goes too far, the harm he causes doesn't bother him as much as being found out and criticized does, which makes him want to fool you even more to further protect his bullshit from being exposed. Although few people can cause you as much harm as a con man, it's not personal. He will say—and truly believe—that he let you down because you don't believe in him or because unavoidable circumstances prevented him from keeping his promises. That's what makes him, technically, an Asshole who can't be helped by shrinks or anyone else. In his mind, his problems are always someone else's fault.

People who love a con man will often rationalize that he just needs professional help and lament that he won't accept it. In truth, professional help has nothing to offer him. A shrink can help his victims and relatives, however, by reminding them that the damage they experience isn't personal, trying to get through to the Asshole or save him will only make it worse, and protecting themselves is a far more important priority.

Charisma can generate excitement and success in a marriage or family, but a spark is not a stable thing on which to build a marriage; charisma also bears a special risk of addiction, disloyalty, and deception. What you hope is that your charismatic partner's character is strong enough to make your relationship worthwhile and, sometimes, to make change possible.

What you must accept, unfortunately, is that charismatic people sometimes lack the strength for commitment and your relationship will be dangerous and always on the brink of combustion. Understanding the risks and benefits of charisma can help you deal with its influence, guide you toward constructive management, and, hopefully, keep things from blowing up or burning out.

### Did You Know . . . Truth, or Bullshit?

*We examine widely accepted beliefs about relationships to determine whether they're true (or not so much). The phrase in question:*
"If I don't find someone, I'll die alone."

If you do not find someone to marry or some fellow olds to split a house and a lanai in Miami with, you will be alone. But that doesn't mean you should give a shit.

First of all, it's important to remember that life is long and death is short, so focusing on the latter over the former is as misguided as paying attention to the quality of the wedding rather than that of the marriage. Sure, it's hard to grow old by yourself, but unless you're living on a space station or in a crazy-brains cat hive, you probably have family, friends, or even former coworkers who have your back or could help you find services that offer support.

So if your search for a partner is motivated by the desperate need for companionship that will be there at the end, you may be forgetting the eons due to pass between your average wedding and average croaking; most people will drive you crazy or ruin your life if you partner up with them, and you're better off enjoying your time on earth with friends and your own company than marrying some schmuck because he's the least schmucky schmuck you can find to protect you from oblivion.

Second, to quote a line from the cult sci-fi series *Firefly*, "Everyone dies alone" (and fun-time lines such as that might explain why it was canceled so quickly). Whether or not you have a companion by your deathbed, or explode along with everyone else on the bus as it hits the beach by the cliff, or drink the Fresca at the same time as a hundred other Xuxu worshippers, the journey into the next world is always solo. Having a spouse won't make dying that different, particularly if he goes first.

There are a lot of good reasons to partner up, but the focus should be on whether partnership improves your life, not your demise.

VERDICT: TOTAL BULLSHIT

A strong person learns how to manage charisma, whether she has it or her spouse does, without its affecting her integrity or weakening her relationships. A weaker person, however, runs into problems without realizing that the personal charm that attracts many kinds of good luck has also burdened her with distraction, unusual responsibilities, and intense temptations. Your burden, when confronting charisma in yourself or someone else, is to be carefully selective in spite of feeling extra attracted, understood, and special. Then you'll know whether you can tame the risks of charisma, bear the temptations it creates, and use it to enrich your life and the life you build with someone else.

| What to Look For | What to Achieve/What Not to Be Fooled By |
| --- | --- |
| Mutual attraction | . . . based on feeling you're interested in each other and reasonably comfortable, and not because you both feel you're in the presence of the most fascinating person in the world. |
| Mutual respect | . . . because you can understand and appreciate each other's strengths and accomplishments, not because you appreciate that one of you has the power to woo anyone and the other had the power to join the woo-er in matrimony. |
| Shared effort | . . . doing things together that are annoying, frustrating, and smelly, rather than working together to be the life of every party (and brunch, bris, wake, etc.). |
| Common interests | . . . in hobbies, friends, and child rearing, and not in the joys of winning friends and influencing people. |
| Common goals | . . . such as being good people, maintaining a stable household, and doing your part to put less plastic in the ocean, and not about being the most interesting couple in the world (as a rule of thumb, any goal that's even loosely affiliated with a beer ad is a bad idea). |

# Five Reasons Good People Can't Find Good Partners

5. *You're too nice:* Again, you'd think being too mean would be more of a problem, but it's worse if you always feel responsible for whatever goes wrong on a date, or for making sure everyone's having fun, or for the weather or the universe in general. Then the bad dates, storms, and luck wear you down until you just want to be left alone to screw up in peace.

4. *You're a woman:* That's right—from haircuts to health care, being a woman is expensive, but your gender is also costing you a decent chance at finding a partner. That's because there are more marriage-qualified women than marriage-qualified men—a little-known clinical fact, but an obvious fact to any woman who's had multiple blind dates show up to a nice dinner in flip-flops—so lots of good women are left without a chair to sit on when the proverbial music stops.

3. *You connect too easily or hang on too long:* You'd think that being a gifted bonder would help if you're looking for lasting love, but not if you attach too easily to people you don't know well or hang on too long to partners who are obvious wastes of time. So you spend too much time talking to, caring for, and dating people who may be nice but aren't your cup of tea. Then, after the breakup, you're not just heartbroken, but are too exhausted and burned-out to get out there and search for someone worthwhile.

2. *You're an oddball:* Sure, it's easier for not-normal people to find each other now that the Internet exists and Comic Con has

worldwide prestige, but anyone whose nerd-dom goes deeper than a pair of glasses and a *Star Wars* T-shirt can tell you that it's never easy for an oddball living in a normal world. Even if you're living among your kind in an artsy city such as Portland or Austin, you're still probably better at collecting small metal figurines than making small talk. Or maybe you're just a lady or dude of average tastes who lives in a different country, or just around a different culture, where you feel totally out of place and unable to connect with anyone, let alone someone you want to connect with in the biblical sense.

1. *You're unlucky:* On the one hand, bad luck invites more bad luck, so not only do people treat you as if you were contagious and deserving of quarantine, but you're too down to prove them wrong. When you're already depressed, broke, or ten pounds over fighting weight, it's nearly impossible to chitchat, laugh at jokes, or even look strangers in the eye, so meeting new people isn't just a struggle, it's torture. On the other hand, you can be going about your search with a positive attitude and a careful approach, and even then, your luck may be garbage and your dates total duds. Bad luck can strike any of us, no matter who we are or what we're like, but don't take it personally or let it push you into settling for an equally bad someone.

# Chapter 2

# F*ck Beauty

Most of us are taught from an early age not to be superficial and overvalue good looks; we're told the parable of the ugly duckling, we're instructed not to judge books by their covers, we're advised to value inner beauty over the outer kind. Unfortunately, our well-meaning teachers and parents are no match for advertising, entertainment, and our own base instincts, which are constantly making the stronger argument that being good-looking is the key to happiness and success.

It's hard to resist the effect that attractive physical attributes have on the way we behave; our brains respond to good and ugly looks in ways that we don't control. Denying the primal power of beauty can be dangerous. You need to manage these feelings, just as you need to manage the primal urge to murder people who cut in line at the post office.

So, even if we know that appearances should not play an important role when we look for love, we can't stop wanting to be perceived

as being attractive and to find an attractive mate, often at our own
peril.

The biggest danger is that beauty may draw us to the wrong person, or that ugliness will prevent us from considering, or being
considered as, a match for a relationship. This makes the already
difficult job of finding a partner even more difficult and has the
added bonus of possibly making you hate the way you look or resent
anyone who's better looking. In other words, having an unremark-
able (or remarkably ugly) appearance doesn't just make it hard to
find an accepting partner, it can make it nearly impossible to accept
yourself, period.

It's especially hard for an online dater to reach out to an unattractive person, no matter how sensible one's intentions, given that
some apps are based entirely on looks (and the dating candidate's
proximity to a tiger, puppy, or sunset). The result is that everyone,
model and civilian alike, doctors photos, believing that it's better to
get lots of responses to a faked photo than none to an honest one,
forgetting that a relationship born from bullshit rarely lasts longer
than a single cup of coffee.

Often, we can find possible partners through work, common
interests, or a matchmaking friend, and once the power of good
talk and compatible personal chemistry takes over, looks become
less important. City life often gets in the way of such opportunities,
however, by creating singles scenes that do nothing but emphasize
the power of attractiveness.

Understanding and accepting the effect appearance has on others
and you is essential if you are to prevent that influence from screwing up your partner search.

We do not believe that improving your looks will help you find
a soul mate, so this chapter doesn't offer any diet tips, makeover
ideas, or do-it-yourself plastic surgery suggestions. Instead, we

urge you to manage how you feel about appearances as you search for a good relationship, even if you have to rein in your natural instincts. To paraphrase the old saying about being thin, looking good feels good, but nothing feels as good as being with someone who won't dump you if you gain ten pounds or wear your sweatpants to bed.

## The Good Things You Want Beauty to Deliver

- A feeling of confidence that comes from being desired, listened to, and envied by those less genetically gifted than you.
- A lot of party invitations, job interviews, and random people wanting to give you free meals, shoes, and cruise ship vacations.
- A date with a good-looking person in a good-looking setting with lots of good-tasting food (that neither of you will eat).
- A confirmation that, by having a stunner on your arm, you're special—a winner with a human trophy to prove it.
- A constant reminder that, no matter how much you hate yourself, you must be doing something right to have bagged such a hot spouse.

## Profile of the Beautiful Ones

Here is a list of traits associated with someone who's irresistibly attractive:

- *Physical attributes:* This one's obvious, although being hot also gives one more confidence, which can affect one's attitude, treatment of others, etc. If she's bought the hype of good looks, she might be extra polished, with a hair/nail/tan/designer-shoe combination that takes more maintenance and costs more than your house.

- *Common occupations:* Aside from the obvious (modeling, personal training, working a makeup counter at Bloomingdale's), there are also the less obvious but equally looks-based sales positions, such as hostess at a fancy restaurant, a pharmaceutical sales rep, or high-powered anything, from lawyer to surgeon, because an ambitious, smart, good-looking person is so unstoppable that you can only hope she's using her power for good.
- *What attracts you first:* If it's not the face or the body, it's being with the kind of person who attracts a crowd drawn to her face and body, or the confidence of that face and body as she handles the crowd.
- *Red flags:* You begin to suspect that said face and body have no actual soul behind them or, even worse, that even after you give up on finding a soul (or just a single thing you and this person have in common), you don't seem to care.

## Seeking Beauty

Unless you're infiltrating an enemy military base or a bank vault or a spot between parked cars for toilet purposes and want people to look the other way, looking good has many advantages. Without having a cult leader or a tribal obligation in common, it's nearly impossible for you to start a relationship if people don't find you attractive enough to talk to, and it's hard to feel genuinely interested in chatting up someone who's ugly. But it's equally impossible to maintain a relationship with someone whose only positive quality is his looks, or to be yourself in a relationship when looks are the glue that holds you two together. Learn to recognize the vulnerabilities and problems unique to a looks-based relationship so you can either find a fix or a less superficial arrangement.

Here are three examples:

- *I had to screw up my courage to talk to this beautiful girl I saw at the bar, but I did, and it's awesome because now we're going out and all the guys look at her and envy me for being her boyfriend. My problem is that I'm still nervous that I'll say something dumb and she'll lose interest, even though she's nice and seems to like me. My goal is to gain enough confidence so I can be myself with her and figure out whether we have a real relationship and whether it's going to work.*

- *I love my boyfriend—he's hotter than the sun and works out even harder than I do—but I'm not the only girl who notices how hot he is, so I'm constantly dealing with jealousy, insecurity, and the urge to punch these bitches who I'm sure are trying to steal him from me. He's not a player, and I don't want to be the kind of girl who needs to be reassured all the time, but going out with him drives me so crazy sometimes that I think I'm going to end up in jail. My goal is to get rid of the jealousy monster inside and stop worrying that he's too hot to want to be with just me.*

- *I've been dating a model, and it's funny, but she's more insecure than I am. She's always worrying about whether her looks are good enough to get her better jobs, and she's always dieting, and she's more preoccupied with her appearance than I am, except in a negative way. She's also constantly telling me how much she likes being with a "normal" (i.e., not model) guy, and how much she envies my normal life, and I don't get why she chooses to live otherwise. I genuinely like her because she's funny and smart*

*(but could probably stand to gain a few pounds), but if she even*
*suspects she's gaining an ounce, she loses her mind. My goal is to*
*figure out how to give her more confidence, so she can enjoy her*
*attractiveness inside and out.*

For those people who are less than secure about their appearance, the yearning for beauty can be constant and unsettling. It
always hurts when you're exposed to the things you want but can't
have—such as when you bike through the perfect neighborhood
you can't afford to live in, or gaze upon a delicious-looking meal
you're deathly allergic to, or fondle beautiful shoes that never come
in sizes big enough for your Sasquatch feet—but it's more painful
to be around something you want to *be* but never will. The closer
you get to people who embody beauty, the more distanced you feel
from yourself.

You'd wish that love, psychotherapy, or a stiff drink could give
you the confidence to feel comfortable and natural with how you
look. That the right eyeliner, surgery, or excruciating undergarment
could mold you into the person you want to see. The truth is, however, that sometimes you can't control beauty or beauty-induced
anxiety, and straining to find the necessary confidence can make
you feel more helpless and stupid.

Yes, sometimes Valium or a drink may help (but never at the
same time). But if they don't, remember that your goal isn't to be
confident. Instead, your goal is to accept your uncomfortable anxiety and self-alienation and still try to get to know someone, hoping
that a real relationship will eventually give you the confidence you
need.

If, after beginning a relationship with someone beautiful, your
anxiety doesn't get better, you may well feel you're about to ruin
something special. In actuality, however, anxiety doesn't mean a

relationship is flawed or doomed to fail; it's a normal and potentially helpful response to the reality that all relationships carry risk, that falling in love can cause heartbreak, and that a bad marriage can cause much worse. So instead of fearing that anxiety will ruin things, give yourself credit for courage, go slow, and keep trying to find things you both enjoy doing and talking about.

Remember, you're not just trying to make a good impression or even play above your weight, you're also trying to learn the basics about her character and prevent attractiveness from drawing you into a truly terrifying mistake. As long as you're willing to endure anxiety while getting to know her better, time will allow you to focus on who she is, not how pretty she is (or how pretty you think you aren't).

For some people, the toxic effect of dating a good-looking person includes jealousy; instead of just feeling goofy and outmatched, you're obsessed, suspicious, angry, and watchful. At just the time you're trying to talk yourself into feeling more confident, you're confronted with internal ugliness you can't stop and certainly can't be proud of.

When beauty makes you feel ugly, your goal isn't to discover your own inner beauty and achieve peace, because, outside of romantic comedies and the godlike powers of RuPaul, that's usually beyond your control. It's to try to act reasonably when what you want to do is prod, read his every text/email/Facebook message, and fish for reassurance. Don't hold yourself responsible for feeling jealous, but do hold yourself responsible for not *acting* jealous. Yes, keeping it inside is painful, but expressing it is worse and will make things ugly for everyone.

If you decide a relationship is worth the pain of jealousy, learn to live with it. Distract yourself by keeping busy, and schedule more alone time together when you feel distanced and don't want to risk the distraction of jealousy. Find positive activities to bring you together, rather than fighting and making up. If you can bear the pain of jealousy without letting it change what you say and do with someone, you're a strong person who can develop a real relationship, even when good looks and jealous feelings make it hard.

Another kind of beauty toxicity for the looks-obsessed, regardless of how beautiful you are, is the compulsion to compare yourself to an impossible standard and worry about all the ways you deviate from the ideal. It's natural, if you're dating such an aesthetically oriented person, to hope that a supportive relationship will ease her fears and allow her to think happier thoughts and share conversations about other topics. Unfortunately, beauty obsession, like anorexia, is not just a form of compulsive insecurity. If she can't trust the mirror, she can't trust logic; no matter how honest and positive you are with your girlfriend, it isn't going to help.

Instead, observe how well she can put aside her body obsessions and care about things that are more important, from what movie the two of you are going to see to who's running for president. If she can't, move on, no matter how exciting it is to date a model, or how sweet and smart you believe her to truly be. You have no power to change her, and you need to find someone who, beautiful or not, can function well as a partner and not let obsession of any kind eclipse her values and take over her life.

People will never stop seeking beauty, in themselves and others, and can drive themselves crazy in the search. Remember why you're dating, however, and stick to your game plan; if you're just out for arm candy, that's one thing, but if, like most people who aren't awful, do have souls, and don't own yachts, you want a fully balanced meal of partnership, then you need to see the bigger, sometimes less pretty picture.

*Quiz: Pondering Prettiness—Are you too attractive,*
*or pretty in need of a new grooming routine?*

1. If your tire goes flat on the highway during morning rush hour,
   you would:
   A: Expect that if you get out of your car a guy (or a party Jeep
      full of them) will soon pull over to offer assistance, try to
      impress you with feats of strength, propose marriage, etc.
   B: Call AAA and have the tow truck driver accuse you of being a
      homeless squatter in your own car because you haven't show-
      ered in a few days and you have a front seat full of Wendy's
      carnage.
   C: If you can't change it yourself, call AAA and tell a sob story
      to the tow truck driver so he'll drop you off at home and save
      you the taxi fare.

2. When you go to weddings and prepare to hit the dance floor,
   your plan is to:
   A: Stand up at your table and wait a few seconds for some
      bridesmaids to drag you onto the dance floor into the center
      of their grind circle until you make a convincing excuse for
      them to let you take a break (and then covertly take the cutest
      one to the bathroom to make out).
   B: Stand around by yourself because no one seems to want to
      dance with you, maybe because of the large wine stain on
      your suit that you didn't notice when you put it on, on the
      bus, because you thought this wedding was next month and
      planning mistakes were made.
   C: Stand around by yourself until you find a girl you're pretty
      sure isn't married or a relative to ask to dance, and she
      says yes, but not for long unless you find something to talk

about over Cover Me Not-Badd, the loud Color Me Badd cover band.

3. During those moments when you just need to get laid, your best course of action is to go to a bar with your best wingwomen and:
   A: Struggle to find a guy (of the many that approach you) who isn't too overeager, too nervous, or too creepy to even share airspace with, let alone naked times.
   B: Curse yourself for forgetting to wear deodorant, then try to find some guy who's just the right amount of drunk (i.e., who can complete sentences, stand upright, or just retain consciousness).
   C: With your friends' help and approval, find a guy who seems to be reasonably competent, not a serial killer, and unlikely to mistake your signals for love.

4. When you're leading a meeting at work, the best way to keep things efficient and professional is to:
   A: Use PowerPoint, stick carefully to an agenda, and keep the lights low for as long as possible; well-lit free discussion just turns all the guys flirty and gets everything way off track.
   B: Memorize a speech, remember not to be too twitchy or pick at anything, and maybe ask your adorable young assistant to help you since she seems to hold everyone's attention.
   C: Learn the material inside and out, structure a strong agenda, and pitch a smart proposal that they'd be stupid to refuse.

5. Upon returning from France, you get busted by customs for accidentally bringing in that cheese you purchased in Normandy but forgot to eat. You deal with the situation by:
   A: Apologizing profusely, begging forgiveness, and quietly

thanking Jebus that you got a female inspection officer who is more than willing to give you a pass and buy you a drink.

B: Get through after some extensive questioning and surviving the humiliating comment that you smell so much like the cheese that you almost got it through.

C: Smile, show your passport, and expect a short set of questions and the loss of some delicious cheese.

If you answered mostly A's . . .

You enjoy the perks of being good-looking, but then get passive when the enthusiasm of the beauty-struck gets in the way of your doing business; you appreciate all the attention and favor your face gets you, but you resent when people expect something in return. You're ready to use your good genes/nose/tush to take advantage of others, which is a good way to become a bad person. If you want your character to match your figure, push yourself to rely less on your looks and take less from other people, even if you're giving them good face.

If you answered mostly B's . . .

Instead of being fixated on looks, you're oblivious of them; you don't notice the way physical repulsiveness can drive people away or make them hostile, unavailable, and hard to deal with. Without much effort, you could probably learn how to avoid absolute ugliness and improve your life. You may never be a supermodel, but with a little work, learning how to pay attention to stains, smells, and the importance of a daily shower, you can be noticed more for who you are than how you look as if you slept under a rock.

If you answered mostly C's . . .

You've found a way to be attractive, and to appreciate beauty in general, without allowing it to dominate your interactions, interfere with business, or pull you toward unworthy relationship candidates, expensive beauty products, and unsafe surgery. Attractiveness often takes work, and limiting its impact takes more work, so keep up the good job because you seem to be pretty adept at doing both.

## Did You Know . . . Dating Someone Ugly on the Outside but Pretty Within Is Just as Dangerous as the Opposite?

Deep down, we all want to be the kind of person who doesn't judge a book by its cover; some take these values even further, wishing to be so unsuperficial and genuine that they could fall for people based solely on the quality of their heart, not the cuteness of their face. This is a particularly attractive idea to those who feel guilty about being physically overgifted, tend to take in stray animals that look as if they've been through a garbage disposal, and/or wish to prove their superiority over a disgustingly commercial, beauty-obsessed culture.

In the dream world of teen movies, YA fiction, and the kind of reality shows that make you stupider as you watch them, this looks/personality discrepancy is solved with a new haircut, pair of contacts, or laser-based inpatient surgery that turns ugly into beautiful. But in real life, if you meet people you click with platonically but without any chemical attraction, then nothing—not taking off their glasses or the mole off their cheek—is going to make you attracted to them, and it will end badly.

For any number of reasons—guilt, desperation, or that sincere wish to see inner beauty win over all external faults—you may be tempted, despite your lack of attraction, to try to make it work physically with someone you like but don't yearn to touch. But being with people you're not physically into, no matter how pretty they are inside, is just as stupid as dating someone who's a gorgeous jerk.

Unfortunately, sexual chemistry, as fickle and unfair as it can sometimes be, is a key element to building relationships, at least at first. As time goes by and a shared relationship becomes a shared life, that chemistry can become less important; but starting from a place of low or no chemistry is basically beginning with a death spiral.

Yes, it's unfair to deny a chance for romance to a good friend based on appearance and sexual chemistry alone, and you can rationalize that being with him is good for him and better for you than being single. It's more unfair, however, to give that friend a chance and then discover, for reasons you don't control, that you can't give the full amount of affection he deserves.

As gross as it is to only judge prospective mates by their physical attributes, it's just as inadvisable to become romantic with someone who seems like a good match when physical attraction isn't there. If you're looking for a long-term partner, avoiding romance with someone you're not sexually attracted to isn't superficial, it's smart.

## Being Beautiful

Over time, getting admiration for good looks may give you special confidence, but it may also give you attention from people who don't know, understand, or like you as you really are. As a result, you may feel hollow and unmotivated to develop skills and achievements that don't involve pictures, partying, and being pawed by a looks-obsessed horde. So, unless you're vain or think being an object is your calling, expect good looks to impose burdens and potentially interfere with your finding true friendship and satisfaction in your life. Learn how to screen out the response that beauty inspires in others, and certainly never depend on it; otherwise, you won't find people who appreciate you for you, and you won't be fully appreciating yourself, either.

Here are three examples:

- *I started to get attention for my looks in junior high, but even after all this time, I'm still not comfortable with it. I think it helped me avoid being bullied in school for being gay, and it certainly makes it easier to meet other guys. But now I also get a lot of attention I don't want or need from people who get hurt if I'm not nice to them or don't give them a lot of attention. People also assume weird things about me based on my looks, like that I'm promiscuous or stupid. It just gets distracting and embarrassing. My goal is to figure out how to keep good looks from ruining my life and making me an asshole.*

- *I'm comfortable with my looks—I'm not a supermodel, but, being frank, men tend to consider me beautiful—and I'm careful not to be overly flirtatious. Still, I've always felt other girls don't trust me because they think I'm trying to steal their dates. I wonder if I'm being more seductive than I realize, but I really do make an effort to keep my signals clear. In the meantime, I miss having closer friendships and being able to hang out with friends who are dating one another. My goal is to get other women to trust me in spite of my good looks.*

- *I've always been known for my good looks, and I've made the most of it as a lifelong bachelor, but I'm afraid I don't have anything else to offer. Now that I'm nearing forty, gaining weight, and losing hair, people are less interested in what I have to say and I'm losing my confidence and starting to panic. My goal is to find an identity and confidence that don't depend on my looks.*

Although we like to think our identities come from who we are more than from the way other people think of us, most of us are, indeed, strongly influenced by how others respond, particularly when we see them every day for a long time. That's why high school often teaches us more about what stereotype we supposedly fulfill than it does about algebra. And why dreamy football players are treated like royalty while zitty, awkward geniuses are often deemed deserving of physical punishment.

When people respond to our good looks, in high school or in the real world, their strong feelings can shape how we see ourselves unless we are strongly grounded or totally oblivious of human interaction. And even if the good-looking are also aware of their good fortune, that doesn't mean that they're immune to an attractiveness backlash.

One dark side of people's response to your good looks, after they've given you attention and flattery, is to find and invent faults that will help soothe their envy. So it's not unusual for people who begin by overadmiring you to soon suspect you of being shallow, promiscuous, and/or incompetent at everything other than a beauty contest. Meanwhile, they discount and ignore your actual gifts or disregard your actual needs, while expecting an unreasonable amount from you and spreading an unrealistic perception of who you are.

Trying to change your image or address the issue by talking about it are two strategies that are usually ineffective; prejudices are powerful, and defensiveness often gives more power and validation to false opinions. You did nothing to cause overly positive and negative judgments other than be attractive, and short of gaining fifty pounds or giving yourself a Trump do, you can probably do little to talk others into seeing beyond your looks to who you really are.

Instead, try to ignore your appearance while focusing on the quality of your work and your relationships with old friends and family. If you're thick-skinned and socially adept, you may achieve this goal while accepting invitations to date, party, and whatever. But if you're sensitive, worry about hurting others, and can't easily say no, be careful. You're better off spending more time at school or the office and restricting your social life until time brings you relationships with people who see you and appreciate you for who you are.

Even if you're comfortable with your good looks and immune to gossip, you may well find yourself isolated from friends who have paired off and are susceptible to insecurity and the fear that you'll seduce their partners. That could cause you to wonder what you did to arouse their fears and try harder to win their trust, but again, your efforts will probably fail. Not only are their fears beyond your control, but you can't correct behavior in yourself that wasn't wrong in the first place.

Instead, accept the paradoxical fact that beauty often makes you lonely, even as it seems to draw people to you, and that you must learn to bear this loneliness without blaming yourself for social mistakes or beauty opportunism. Respect yourself for living up to your standards, regardless of temptation, and for tolerating lonely times without lowering your friendship standards.

If you find yourself worried that age will strip away your looks—and a beauty-driven lifestyle—don't assume that you're losing something of great value or, worse, the only thing you own. You may indeed have come to depend on the pleasures of sexual conquest, admiration, and special treatment. The alternative, however, is not to be ordinary, ignored, and forever alone.

Being born with good looks has probably delayed your ability to accept what's not so beautiful in other people and so develop deeper relationships. As a result, enjoying the pleasures of attractiveness can make long-term relationships look dull and ugly. And it's true that no one seems beautiful when you're both tired and arguing about whose turn it is to buy more toilet paper.

Your goal, when beauty fades, is to ignore your withdrawal symptoms and seize the opportunity to start growing. Work with a good therapist or coach to figure out how to accept your new normal life, and respect yourself for doing a good day's work and being decent to others, even though you miss having a great head of hair. If you can ignore the way you feel and retrain yourself to respect values that depend on who you are and how you act, you can also build relationships that increase in value with age, even as your own reflection becomes less prized.

Having beauty may win you admiration and dates, but it can cause you to miss opportunities to find respect and real love. Instead of blaming yourself if it causes you trouble, learn to tolerate its burdens and not overvalue its pleasures. Then you can graduate to enjoying your appearance without letting it interfere with your ability to work hard, be a decent person, and find real beauty—not in the mirror or the approval of your peers, but in family, long-term relationships, and hard-earned moments of happiness.

## Appearance Improvement Techniques: Pros and Cons

| Technique | Pro | Con |
|---|---|---|
| Weight loss | Done carefully, i.e., without straight-up starving yourself or just drinking lemon juice and tears for a month, you might be helping your heart, avoiding diabetes, and improving your health overall. Plus, exercise is proven to help your mood (assuming you don't pull, break, or tear something important). | Being thinner won't automatically make you more confident—your body absorbs food, but your personality does not—nor does it instantly give you the ability to deal with an influx of attention, especially the kind that comes from people who are homing in on your new "hot" body type. Ew. |
| Plastic surgery | It's a surefire way to approach anything about your body that you can't hide or accept. Plus, it can stop that pesky snoring once and for all. | It's a big risk (RIP, Kanye's mom) without a big guaranteed reward, because as much as it feels as if your life would be better if you just had bigger lips or boobs or biceps, that's rarely how it works. Plus, again, the new attention can be tough because, while you might have hated being flat before, you probably won't enjoy being a magnet for tit-obsessed creeps now. |

| Technique | Pro | Con |
|---|---|---|
| Style makeover | Taking a chance on a new haircut, wardrobe, and/or eyebrows can be scary, but you don't have that much to lose (except your gross old clothes), and it's certainly less risky than joining a cult gym or getting your face sliced open. | Your stylist might make a major misstep, and bangs and eyebrows take a long time to grow out (and pictures of you dressed like an idiot with bad bangs or clown brows last forever). Most important, you can't assume you're a different, better person just because your face got plucked. |
| Therapy | If you want to prettify your insides as well as your exterior, talking to someone about your relationship priorities and the hurdles you face is a good step. | A therapist can help coach you through dating, but can't help you become a more dateable person or perform an exorcism. If you go seeking a new you instead of useful advice, you're in trouble. |
| Finding religion | Can help some people get their lives in order, even if they're not in jail. | Religion brings people together, but if your passion for Xenu is the main thing keeping you and your spouse together, you'll be sorry. |

## Marriage and Beauty

Marriage may solve some problems for the overly good-looking; in spite of the shallow pleasures and temptations of being admired, you've found someone with whom you want to share a deep commitment. If you've become dependent on your good looks for fun and self-esteem, however, marriage can bore you, challenge your feelings of being special, and trigger withdrawal symptoms. Unless you're relatively oblivious of the way people react, the transition from being admired and serially dated to being taken for granted by a loving spouse can be a painful lesson. Still, it's worth pushing through because if you can't kick your craving for shallow admiration, the realities of marriage will create more problems than they solve.

Here are three examples:

- *I was always attracted to my husband—he's not a hunk or anything, but my kind of cute. Ten years into our marriage, however, he's gained some weight, grown some hair in weird places, and generally stopped looking in the mirror, so I'm just not that into him physically anymore. I can't help it, but it takes away the sexual pleasure of our marriage, and I resent his inability to do the least bit of maintenance, especially since I'm slathering myself in antiaging cream and counting all my steps. My goal is to get him to take better care of himself so we can keep our marriage from becoming sexually boring.*

- *My wife is losing her looks, but after three pregnancies and many years of marriage, that's just what happens. No matter how many times I reassure her that I don't care how her body's changed and would love her even if she grew a full mustache, her changed appearance bothers her and gets her depressed. That makes her grouchy with me and the kids, and that's much more of a problem than her weight. My goal is to get her to see that looks don't matter and make her feel better.*

- *My wife always puts a huge effort into making herself look good, which I thought was fine when we were dating, but now, ten years later, she puts the same amount of effort in. The only difference*

*is now she doesn't just care about how she looks, but about how I
and the kids present ourselves, and all the crap she makes us do
before we're allowed to leave the house is driving us all crazy. My
goal is to get her to relax her focus on appearances before we all
get too mad at her and rebel.*

Most people aren't foolish enough to marry someone based solely on his or her looks; like buying oceanfront property on an eroding cliff or getting a tattoo celebrating a Patriots Super Bowl victory before the season starts, it's almost certain to be a doomed investment. In addition to being superficial and sure to fade, good looks may also create needs and expectations within a marriage that are so hard to deal with that they last longer than the good looks themselves.

There's nothing wrong, for example, with finding your husband handsome and, as a result, sexually attractive. If you were lucky, you wouldn't care when aging made him look mature, distinguished, or, to be less tactful and positive, lumpy and gross. Unfortunately, sexual attraction is delicate and unpredictable, regardless of what lady-magazine writers and even animal biologists tell you, mostly because they only cover courtship rituals. Keeping up interest after the flirtation ends and the bright plumage fades is much more complicated, unpredictable, and uncontrollable.

In spite of your determination to eat and live healthily and invest in a close relationship, libido can suddenly disappear because of stress, aging, negative appearance, or some other cause that no one can diagnose. Not that a diagnosis matters, because even if you know why you feel the way you do, you can never control how or why you are or aren't attracted to someone. So if you prod your partner to change or make it clear that your sexual satisfaction is on the line, you may find yourself with conflict, diminished performance, and more frustration. After all, he could hit the gym, hire a personal stylist, and even develop a signature scent, and you might still find yourself not interested anymore. Then the only physical thing you'll want to do with each other is bare-knuckle box.

Accept that, without your being a shallow person, his appearance was more of a sexual trigger than you realized and that now it's not so hot and may never get better. Certainly, his appearance and your response to it are not under your control, so restoring his attractiveness is a lousy goal. Instead, review the parts of your marriage that work well. Hopefully, you can reassure yourself that your marriage has brought you much more than has been lost by the decline in sexual pleasure, so you don't feel like a victim.

Then, when your resentment is well hidden, ask him whether he's interested in improving his health with diet and exercise. Offer to help by changing the foods you buy, your menu, and your schedule of activities. If you accept him the way he is and thus take failure off the table, you may be able to help him get healthy and get back that bonus. If you can't accept that his looks aren't likely to improve, think of what you've gained from your partnership. Of course, if you've lost more than you've gained, you may have good reason to move on. Otherwise, remember that you chose a good partner, built a good marriage, had fun while the sex was hot, and now it's time to make the best of something that can't be helped.

Sometimes a partner may have an intense need to look good, regardless of how much she loves you. Although focusing exclusively on beauty can make one shallow, many people care deeply about work and relationships and still can't get good looks off their mind. Maybe beauty-mindedness is a kind of OCD; if so, it's not uncommon and may confer a Darwinian survival advantage on those who have it genetically programmed into their brains. Even so, living with someone's beauty obsession is torture.

Trying too hard to stop your partner from suffering every time she looks in a mirror probably won't work because, as you've learned and as we've previously discussed, reassurance and logic have no effect on compulsive feelings and involuntary thoughts. Pushing her to be happier will backfire if she feels blamed for a response she can't help. So stop wasting time disagreeing with her thoughts, because they're just a compulsion, not credible ideas that even deserve consideration, and the more time you spend trying to refute them, the more you empower them.

Your goal isn't to prove her wrong, but to lovingly push her toward finding a way to keep her thoughts from uglying up your life together. Urge her to remember what she has created in your marriage in spite of her worries. Remind her that she may get relief from treatment or, at the least, ideas on how to distract herself and prevent obsessive thoughts from controlling her behavior. If nothing helps, take comfort from your own good efforts and do what you can to protect yourself from her negativity. Regardless of her self-torturing thoughts, you know you have a good marriage and that she's been a good wife and mother. Your hope is that she'll share your perspective, even when her thoughts tell her otherwise.

If your partner's beauty preoccupations know no boundaries and force her to fuss about your and your children's appearance, then you have more reason to resent her obsessions and wish she could change. You're sorry she's making herself miserable, but it's hard not to resent feeling controlled and criticized. Unfortunately, you are up against an additional hard-to-change trait—her tendency to see family as a part of herself—so trying to get her to stop will probably trigger more conflict. Perhaps a family therapist will referee, tell her that she's going too far, and offer validation. Change, however, may still be hard to come by, particularly if she sees the therapist as having taken your side.

If you can't change your partner, build better boundaries. Don't respond to conversations about appearances but do talk about good times, growth, and accomplishments. Veto appearance-related activities that you consider too demanding while suggesting alternatives. Don't criticize her views or defend your own, other than to note the difference and express determination to pursue your own course, and for the kids to do the same if they so choose.

Living with the beauty obsessed or with your own beauty obsession doesn't mean that you can't love and enjoy your family and work and share other values. Even if you may have to accept the burdens of living with those obsessions, you never have to believe that the opposite of enjoying beauty is succumbing to ugliness; it's learning to keep your beauty-related feelings contained while working hard to develop the interests, values, and relationships that make life truly beautiful.

Hopefully, marriage will provide you with much more than the opportunity to be a beautiful couple, and if so, you will have strong weapons to keep beauty from controlling or interfering with your lives, or ruining your investment in your life together.

**Did You Know . . . Truth, or Bullshit?**

*We examine widely accepted beliefs about relationships to determine whether they're true (or not so much). The phrase in question:*
"There's someone for everyone."

The notion that everybody has a soul mate—the one perfect person somewhere on the globe who will make life complete—is harmless in theory, and certainly profitable as the basis for holiday-themed Hallmark "movie events." If taken seriously, however, the belief that you can find the right mate if you just search hard enough can set you up for intense disappoint-ment. Not surprisingly, we believe that finding someone is a gift, not a given, and the search for such a person should be taken seriously . . .

. . . unless, of course, you've got questionable hygiene or mental health and are generally the kind of person any sane, bathed person would cross the street to avoid.

One thing Dr. Bennett learned working in mental hospitals is that the crazier, dirtier, or more feral the patient, the more likely that patient is to have a spouse. A patient who was as psychotic as he was morbidly obese was accompanied by a doting wife, and the woman sent to the loony bin for drinking from public toilets had a devoted husband (and, to the amazement of everyone on the floor, a very white set of teeth). My father's less or not crazy patients—the ones he saw in private practice, outside the mouse-filled walls of the public hospital—were far more likely to be single (and showered and more likely to be considered appealing mates).

It became a joking catchphrase for my father and his coworkers—such as when the patient with a full mustache was being visited by her husband (also with a full mustache)—to smile and say in unison, "There's someone for everyone!" It's almost heartwarming, until you realize how grim it is.

If you believe you've found your soul mate, there's no reason to believe it's just because you're in dire need of psychiatric help or a really hot bath. But if you're looking for that perfect someone, the best way to find him or her is to have the least perfect brain and body odor.

—SB

VERDICT: TOTAL BULLSHIT (UNLESS YOU'RE BONKERS AND/OR DISGUSTING)

Beauty may be skin-deep, but our appreciation of it is deep-wired into our brains, and thus, whether we like it or not, into our values. Whether you want it, have it, or had it, beware its effect on your choices and the feelings that drive them. Those feelings are not linked to your will or good intentions, and when they aren't pushing you to do and say stupid things, often with the wrong people, they're causing hurt, frustration, and obsession. That's why you need to be prepared to recognize your response to beauty, including your own appearance, so that you can ignore it without blaming yourself for its selfishness or irrationality. Indeed, being sensitive to attractiveness and still being able to make good choices about people is a beautiful achievement.

| What to Look For | What to Achieve/What Not to Be Fooled By |
| --- | --- |
| Mutual attraction | . . . based on still liking each other despite a deep acceptance of your ugly moments—yours and your partner's—rather than a love of how good you look together. |
| Mutual respect | . . . because you appreciate how much you and/or your partner have accomplished in spite of how you look, good or bad, rather than because of it. |
| Shared effort | . . . put into accomplishing things that realize your goals but may cause wrinkles, rather than trading beauty and clothing tips and enhancing each other's appearances while avoiding real challenges. |
| Common interests | . . . in what you do with family and friends, rather than in high fashion, skin-care products, and the least amount of calories one can survive on in a day. |
| Common goals | . . . such as making enough money to take care of the kids and cover major disasters, not to fund shopping sprees and full-body tucks. |

# Ten Questions to Which the Answer Is Always No

1. If he's not texting, emailing, calling, or responding to me with anything but stony silence, is there any good reason for me not to take that as a sign he's not interested?

2. Follow-up question: Is it reasonable to assume that a cute girl who doesn't respond is no longer a worthy crush but a vicious cuntzilla whom I should stop reaching out to for dates and start overwhelming with threatening, angry communiqués?

3. If the way to a man's heart is through his stomach, then the way to a woman's heart is through the screen of her phone, especially through a close-up picture of your weenus, right?

4. Is it a good idea, a great idea, or the best idea to get this neck tattoo?

5. Isn't it always noble to stand up to people who've really hurt you, especially if you use the one weapon they're vulnerable to—an honest explanation of what you think about them and how they make you feel, a.k.a. the truth?

6. As an adult, can I still use the "he/she started it" excuse I learned as a kid if I punch a guy who hit me first, or run a car off the road after it cut me off, or slap a girl who won't stop making fun of my poster of Dwayne "The Rock" Johnson?

7. Is it valid to break up with someone using just the emojis of a broken heart, a crying cat, and a beeper?

8. If I want to tell someone something honest yet downright mean, will prefacing my statement with "Don't take this the wrong way" negate all the probable hurt I'll cause?

9. So I don't really need to go to 12-step meetings and join the cult of NA if my ability to recently quit heroin cold turkey clearly proves that I *do* control my addiction and a higher power can suck my dick?

10. Will I, a human male, be more attractive if I grow my hair and wear it in a ponytail?

Chapter 3

# F*ck Chemistry

In the realm of relationship terminology, "chemistry" initially seems like a misnomer. What do mutual interest and attraction have to do with the high school science class with the most bong-able equipment? Then again, given how interpersonal chemistry can be as combustible, toxic, and quick to evaporate as anything you bubbled in a test tube when you were a teenager, the term begins to make sense.

Unlike actual chemistry, however, interpersonal chemistry isn't easily explained in a textbook, or even in this book; nobody knows exactly why certain people are drawn to each other or stay together when they're the human equivalents of chlorine and ammonia. We just believe that, without interpersonal chemistry, a relationship can't exist.

Just because chemistry is necessary, however—it's hard to spend lots of time with someone you are blah about—it's no reason to stay in a toxic relationship. Even if you're good at mixing chemicals and getting solutions to change colors, don't assume that chemistry can be changed or influenced by talk, love, a new haircut, a relaxing weekend together at a cat-themed B and B, or therapy.

In reality, chemistry, both scientific and interpersonal, is essential, dangerous, and made up of elements that can't be changed; it's something we can't ignore or do without. But in relationships, we have little control of it, and in love, as in the development of Oxy-Contin, it often has nothing to do with what's good for us.

It's normal to try to control interpersonal chemistry for maximum results; we want to hit it off with people we're attracted to, who turn out to be good people whom we can get along with and count on forever. What chemistry often does, however, is draw us to the wrong people, stir up our darker selves, and stop us from thinking rationally. We desperately want to believe we can control it—we sometimes pay shrinks for the same reasons we used to buy love potions—and we never want to accept the obvious signs that we can't.

Once you accept that chemistry is what it is, it's not hard to understand where it wants to take you and whether you are getting closer to the kind of relationship and future that you value. That's why you need rules and procedures—not to control the chemistry of a relationship, but to assess its power and remember where you want to go, regardless of where the powerful feelings of interpersonal chemistry are pushing you.

No matter the context, chemistry requires caution; before mixing anything, put on your safety goggles, guard your heart, and hope to do just well enough for that passing grade.

## The Good Things You Want Good Chemistry to Deliver

- A spark so eternal, you could get a job at Arlington National Cemetery.
- A mutual attraction so strong, you'll always want to bone each other, even when you're so old that most of your bones' joints have been replaced.
- A makeover for your personality's least attractive and undesirable attributes.
- A blossoming of your verbal creativity that previous relationships have left dormant.
- A mountain of mutual respect that makes nagging and arguing inconceivable.

## Profile of the Master Chemist

Here is a list of traits associated with the person who triggers rapid, intense chemistry:

- *Physical attributes:* A posture, facial expression, and depth of shirt neckline that magically combine to unlock the desire center of your brain. He also has dry hands (because he'll be touching you as much as he can get away with) and the lingering and intense eye contact of a beagle puppy.
- *Common occupations:* Those that depend on rapid emotional connection, e.g., sales, politics, public relations, exotic dancing. Acting and playing music are also popular occupations of master sparkers, which is to say, being unemployed.
- *What attracts you first:* The earliness and ease with which he shares confidences, the intensity of his attraction to you and

response to your every word and sneeze, the buzz of said intense connection.

- *Early red flags:* His attention is intense but he's as distractible as an infant, he avoids talking about prior relationships because they all ended with police intervention but says it's because he can't think about anyone but you, he refers to himself as a "hopeless romantic" in the same breath that he refers to his desire to attach his abusive ex's balls to his key ring, he says many smart, flattering things but they all sound strangely familiar or rehearsed or taken from the mind of Shonda Rhimes.

## Seeking Chemistry

Since you can do nothing to change a person's character once you're committed to him, even if it's just through a lease or Netflix subscription, your initial selection is critical. Chemistry will try to control your choice, so knowing what creates a spark and then fans the flames is essential to understanding how to improve your odds of finding a good partner and avoiding predictable heartache.

Here are three examples:

- *I know it's a cliché, but I'm always attracted to damaged bad boys, and it never ends well. I just click with them so quickly, before I even realize how broken they are or that I'm fucking up again, and by the time I do realize it, I'm already in major trouble, like we're on the cusp of matching tattoos or we've already signed a lease (on an apartment he'll never pay his share of the rent for). My goal is to break the habit and find a way to be attracted to guys who won't ruin my life.*

- *I'm what they call a permanent resident of "the friend zone"—I'm good at getting close to girls but never getting past friendship. It doesn't make me hate women or anything, just frustrated with myself because I don't know what I'm doing wrong to get stuck in the same position over and over. My goal is to make it clear to the women I'm interested in that I want more than just being friends.*

- *I love the rush of meeting and connecting with interesting, attractive women, but things get boring after I catch them and they're clearly attached to me. I don't like to lie or hurt their feelings, but when the relationship stops being exciting, then the spark seems to disappear and I get restless. My goal is to find someone who makes me feel different or to stop being such a restless person.*

Oh, to be one of the lucky few who have good chemistry with those they attract and are attracted to until they attract someone meant for them (in a film, this is usually a journalist or an architect). Then they go off and buy each other perfect gifts, support each other completely in their careers, and have simultaneous orgasms, so simpatico are they.

The unlucky masses are the people for whom films with that plot are made—those who can't stop dating men who aren't architects but aspiring line cooks, or whose crushes often go unrequited, or who are only attending the movie to be rewarded with marital sex.

Unfortunately, we often feel the strongest, sparkiest chemistry with wild people who don't behave well, can't do their share of the work, and require lots of maintenance. People fall into relationship traps for many reasons, but knowing them won't necessarily help you get free or get over the habit of doing it again and again.

Therapists tell us we have the best chemistry with the worst people because troubled types channel the wild side we don't dare express ourselves or remind us of dear dad before he entered rehab. Magazines tell us (women) it's because we hate ourselves (and that we're so fat and our nails are so busted that we're probably right). Darwin says it's because we inherited weird behavioral genes that surfaced in that creepy uncle who chain-smoked and had a tattoo on his hand. Explanations, however, don't change chemistry, and seeking them holds out false hope that someday you'll feel different and your bad relationship impulses will be gone. Try talking to friends or a therapist about your dead-end attractions if you think it will change them, but don't be surprised if it doesn't. Instead, accept your helplessness and look for new ways of managing feelings that aren't going to change.

Assess the damage done by your relationship blunders and list what you want in life that requires a better partner. Then get coaching from friends or a therapist, spot the situations that lower your resistance to bad choices (e.g., barhopping around Christmas, going stag to weddings, Thursdays), and prepare for a period of disciplined, painful self-frustration. Even when you can't change strong destructive chemistry, you can change your behavior. You just need a good reason and lots of determination.

If, instead, your problem is weak chemistry and you find it hard to strike sparks with anyone you're interested in, make sure it's not for lack of a fashion sense, tact, or deodorant. Often, all you need is a good hairdresser, a kind sibling, or a close female friend (that you don't secretly long for) who can give you some honest advice about what not to say to, wear in front of, or smell like around prospective dates when you're nervous.

Otherwise, you may have to accept that, like the person above, you just don't have good dating chemistry, and there's no point in criticizing yourself or seeking explanations in the hope that they will release your inner sex magnet. Rather, widen your date search while making it clear that you'd like a relationship, not a buddy—searching online or via apps establishes that from the jump—and don't let yourself get bogged down with chums. The usual answer to bad dating chemistry, when simple change isn't possible, is opening yourself up to a wider sample and refining your selection so as to avoid wasting time.

Relationship restlessness is another trait that interferes with any lasting bond; it may turn you into an excellent pickup artist, but also a partner-dropping asshole. Again, searching for understanding and blaming your need for sexual reassurance or mistrust of your mother may be interesting, but it won't make the thrill of the hunt any less alluring.

You may not be ready to curb your restlessness until you're old enough to find little meaning in seduction, or until your usual hunting-party pals are either settling down or drying out. You won't find the strength to change unless you can find a greater value in partnership and family than you do in romance and the special attention you get from a lover. If you do decide to change, then you've got well-tested methods (see above) that can help you. Sticking to these methods won't make you happy in the short run, and your restlessness may well fuel a small power plant if you keep your dating behavior under control. If you do, however, you can find a stable partnership and the satisfactions that go with it.

Yes, sometimes dating chemistry can be improved by a change in wardrobe, a good diction coach, or a strong blow to the head. More often, however, it requires you to remember where you want to be in ten years, to accept the defective dating equipment that God gave you, and to work harder at either finding the right person or controlling the wrong impulse. You may never find your eternal, exciting match, but you'll stop finding yourself in the same emotional mess.

### Quiz: Chemistry for Beginners—How Selective Is Your Sparking?

1. When you think you're into someone, your most tried-and-true flirting technique is to:

   A: Ask her how much she liked *Avengers: Age of Ultron*, whether she likes Joss Whedon's Marvel print or film stuff more, and how she felt about the lack of continuity between Matt Fraction's *Hawkeye* comics and the Hawkeye from the film. If her answers aren't "Kinda," "Neither" (she prefers his Dark Horse output), and "That was bullshit," then she clearly isn't the one.

   B: Put my best foot forward, laugh readily, answer questions with questions, and try not to make that phlegmy noise in my throat that happens during allergy season that my mother says I should get checked out by a doctor already.

   C: Ask a bunch of questions, make enough eye contact to seem friendly and not like I'm recruiting for a cult, and maybe subtly fish for opinions on specific, important things, because if she virulently hates her parents as much as she loves Ayn Rand, I know I need to make a polite escape.

2. You think the clearest signal that someone's returning your interest is:

   A: He and I find each other from across a crowded room and instantly get lost in each other's eyes, thoughts, and hearts, immediately opening up to each other about our hopes, dreams, and secrets, knowing instinctually that we were made for each other and that our wedding colors will be blush, dove, and unicorn blood.

B: He doesn't get that face that looks as if someone farted, or he likes my joke about *Everybody Loves Raymond*, or he sticks around long enough that I know that, when he says he has to go to the bathroom, he probably actually has to pee.

C: We lose track of time having a conversation that's actually interesting, not just flirty and giggly, and also revealing of his character, which, blessedly, seems balanced, not too wimpy, and solid overall. Then he asks for my contact information or generally lays the groundwork for our seeing each other again without being a total slimeball.

3. If you could describe the kind of person you spark with most easily, it would be:

A: Somebody whose favorite movie is (X), favorite book is (Y), shoes are made by (Z) and are a size (W), favorite bachelor ever (from *The Bachelor*) is (V), and blood type is (N)-. Maybe (N)+, but that's pushing it.

B: Someone who looks like she likes me, which is to say, she isn't afraid to stand less than two feet away from me and doesn't seem to be searching for excuses to walk away.

C: I *can* spark with lots of different girls that I think are good-looking or funny or whatever, but I try to only pursue connections with those who have more going on than a nice face, outgoing personality, or jeans that fit.

4. The flirtation is killed when your object of flirtation . . .

A: Doesn't understand why it's so important to me that he also loves diet cherry Dr Pepper or judges me when I'm just trying to be open and honest with him about my feelings and my remorse over accidentally running over an old person with my car.

B: Waits until the end of the evening to introduce me to her boyfriend or her girlfriend, or if she casually asks me if I'm on the autism spectrum.

C: Gives me a good reason to believe he's unstable, unreliable, unintelligent, or only into me because he likes something about my body, or just wants attention from anyone, or is a dreaded creepazoid/nut job.

5. You'd describe the minimum level of sparkage to stay interested as:

A: Shares all of my interests, but maybe less intensely. But makes up for it by hating the same things I do, but more intensely. But is into me most intensely (but maybe not as intensely as I'm into him).

B: Acts friendly even after the first meeting (or is at least willing to acknowledge that we've met before).

C: If she's fairly good-looking, not too boring, smart enough, vaguely thoughtful, not scary . . . I'll agree to coffee maybe, or at least exchange a few texts.

6. Once you hit it off with someone, the next step is to . . .

A: Make sure we are so perfectly aligned that we can get married, start our life together, and enjoy a life of complete sharing (feelings, bank accounts, organs, etc.).

B: Daydream about him constantly, find him on Facebook, and endlessly write and rewrite him the perfect text or G-chat that usually ends up being something like "Hi."

C: Text or email with her, then arrange a meetup that's low pressure and potentially fun.

7. For you to pursue a connection, the initial spark has to . . .

A: Be honest, absolute, and totally committed to the values of intimacy and sharing (specifically, valuing, being intimate with, and sharing time with me).

B: Exist in my own mind.

C: Convince me there's potentially something there.

If you answered mostly A's . . .

You are looking for a chemistry so powerful and sharing so complete that you would save a lot of time by just looking in a mirror, and since you'll likely be alone a lot, you'll have plenty of time to check yourself out. Maybe it's time to consider people who don't immediately knock your socks off or know exactly what kind of socks you like.

If you answered mostly B's . . .

You need to raise your standards, rally your courage, and learn how to be discriminating, even when you're very, very anxious to please. If you fall for every girl who talks to you or every guy who gives you a second look, you end up with lots of empty crushes, painful friendship, and few connections.

If you answered mostly C's . . .

Your approach is a healthy slow-and-steady, even if your results are largely dependent on the frequency of your search, your ability to keep your head up, and the quality of your search pool, because certain places—those with lots of people working in finance or near a university with a nationally televised football program—can be creep city.

## Beware the Permaflirt: How Not to Fall for Someone Who Flirts with Everyone

Like walking in heels, spitting tobacco, and borrowing slang from a different age or ethnic demographic, flirting is a skill that is difficult to master, despite the number of people who do it so effortlessly that it seems like second nature.

For most of us, the goal is to get good enough at flirting that you can talk to someone you're interested in, in a way that makes your interest clear and entices them to reciprocate. Sometimes while standing in stilettos, spitting chaw into an empty beer can, or saying "Knawmean?" as if it were just something that middle-aged white men do.

Yet some people flirt so masterfully, so intently, that one pout directed at a sofa could convince it to move itself upstairs. They are excellent at knowing when to lock eyes, when to laugh, and when to accidentally/not-so-accidentally touch their target's arm. They have these skills, however, because they'll flirt with anyone and anything, including a sofa, even a sofa they don't like.

For them, flirting is second nature; they aren't even doing it on purpose, which means they often unwittingly flirt with people they aren't even interested in. These are the permaflirts, and if you're one of their objects of impersonal flirtation, it can feel like a mindflirtfuck.

The permaflirt's behavior has many possible motivations: a deep-seated insecurity that drives them to woo everyone and anyone so as to boost their flagging confidence; a sociopathic desire to manipulate people for personal gain; or a genuine high from the thrill of connecting with someone, even if they lose interest the second the connection is established. No matter what the cause, the outcome for the duped object of their flirtation is always some mixture of confusion, disappointment, and anger, a.k.a. heartbreak.

The socially awkward or flirting-impaired are usually the most vulnerable to their charms, but permaflirts are so blindly persistent that nobody is safe. Most people don't realize the person they're interested in is a permaflirt until it's too late, i.e., until they've interacted enough to feel mired in mixed messages and relationship riddles. Who likes to laugh and cuddle but not kiss or return your calls? Who is always happy to see you and to have intense conversations but makes no effort to make these meetings happen? Who spends three days doing nothing but talking and being naked with someone just to fall off the face of the earth right afterward? Hint: it's not the sphinx.

Being duped by a permaflirt is painful, but when someone who makes eyes at lampposts isn't really interested in you, take comfort in that the rejection isn't personal. The permaflirt teaches us that, for some people, chemistry isn't always a means to an end; some people flirt well—and flirt in a seemingly earnest manner—for flirting's sake. For your own sake, it's best to take all flirting with a grain of salt until you get to know someone for the permaperson he or she is.

## Having Chemistry

Chemistry changes as you spend more time together and start to respond to your less than ideal, unfiltered, occasionally flatulent selves. What you hope is that familiarity improves your comfort with each other, your ability to joke together, and time you spend together without clothes on. What actually happens is that growing comfort allows you to be your sometimes negative, irritable, avoidant self. If it works out and you don't drive each other crazy, and sometimes even if you do, you enjoy the pleasure of feeling accepted by someone who may not like your negativity, but doesn't take it personally and can ignore it. Otherwise, you discover that your real, natural chemistry brings out the worst in both of you and, regard-less of how attracted you are to each other, is better off being filtered away.

Here are three examples:

- *My boyfriend and I fell for each other instantly, but I think somehow he fell harder for me than I did for him. Now he's so totally devoted that it makes me feel suffocated and turns me off. I feel guilty because he is a nice guy and deserves better, but he won't give me a second to myself or even give me the criticism I deserve. I mean, sometimes I get so fed up that I find myself being mean to him, but even then, he never calls me on it, and it gives me the creeps and makes things even worse. My goal is to find someone who loves me but isn't blind to my faults.*

- *I'm surprised by the amazing physical chemistry I have with my new girlfriend, even though we don't have that much to say to each other or that much in common (I think). We don't have long talks or share personal problems, but we sure don't get tired of seeing each other naked. It makes me wonder whether we've discovered the secret of a lasting relationship, given the many people who fall in love and lose interest in sex after a few years. My goal is a relationship that lasts (I'm not that interested in having kids), and I wonder if this is it.*

- *I love my boyfriend, but I get scared at how angry I get when he pushes my buttons. Sometimes, when he's in a bad mood, he says just the right things to make me furious, and then I serve it right back to him. I don't ever do it but I certainly imagine hitting him, and I know he's wanted to do the same. I just wish we could get rid of the passionate anger part and just keep the passionate love.*

*My goal is to figure out if we should stay together or whether our anger is going to drive us apart.*

Humans have never been very successful at containing or controlling passionate feelings; think of the people who love certain football teams so much they can't help but stand in the freezing cold wearing nothing but body paint, or those who love certain doughnuts so much they consume them until their pants (and arteries) burst.

Why we'd think that strong interpersonal feelings would be easier to control is a mystery. Maturing relationships trigger feelings that are even stronger and harder to suppress than those for college sports. You can't force yourself to love or not love, lust or not lust, or get angry or forget about it. As Ecclesiastes says, there may be a time for all of these things, but the timing is seldom opportune or under your control.

If you find yourself underloving someone who deserves better, your guilt will probably make things even more difficult. You'll try to be kinder, which will make you resentful, and any show of resentment (especially when it's received without complaint) will make you feel guilty, which will trigger more kindness.

Sooner or later, you have to ask yourself whether the chemistry is tolerable without making yourself responsible for or guilty about the pain it causes. You must decide whether your feelings make it possible for you to be with someone and behave like a reasonable friend and partner, or whether you owe it to him to break it off, no matter how much hurt it may cause in the short run. If you choose the latter, then it's time to stop the relationship without blame, self- or otherwise. Respect that you've both made a good effort and, for no reason you can see, the chemistry went bad, and you can do nothing to make it right. Breaking up may feel like a failure, but it's never a failure when it reflects facts that can't be changed.

If your chemistry with someone is strongly physical, it's especially dangerous because then it's based more on actual chemical interactions (i.e., hormones, endorphins, flavored lube, etc.) than on respect, common interests, and an ability to work well together. Good sexual chemistry is like a drug that talks you into having one more hit; it tries to persuade your brain that, having discovered a new favorite pastime, you can now and forever control your happiness.

The reality, however, is that it's hard to spend lots of time with someone you don't like or respect, no matter how much time you spend getting high off each other. If you haven't learned this before, you will now. Don't let wishful thinking interfere with your lesson.

Remember, even if you don't have children, a partnership requires a lot of interaction and working together, and sex doesn't have the power to improve someone's character or make her great to be with. While it may seem like a case of not being able to have your cake and eat it, too, that's not actually the applicable problem or cliché, because in relationships, sexual chemistry is the frosting, not the cake. Don't let lust prevent you from using wisdom and experience to tell you whether a partnership is likely to work.

Occasionally hating the one you love doesn't have to break up a relationship, but it's also not something you can eliminate or avoid, even if you're a devout believer in the power of communication, therapy, and exorcisms. Yes, some misunderstandings can be cleared up. What you're left with, however, particularly with people who love each other and work closely together, is episodic hate that's a part of life.

If that's the case, don't make it worse by trying to eliminate it or blaming yourself or your chosen peacemaker. Instead, ask yourself whether the relationship is worthwhile, rage and all, and whether you have the strength to limit the damage. If it is, become an expert at rage management. Learn how to go to bed angry and without having to have the last word because, despite all advice to the contrary, no fight had while both parties are exhausted is worth having, let alone winning (see the sidebar on p. 106). Develop methods for retreating to a nice quiet hidey-hole when a fight has gone too far. Don't let pain or rage devalue a relationship that, in your quiet moments, you believe is worth the effort.

If rage leads to violence, your job is to protect yourself from a relationship that isn't safe or good for your health. Love, regret, and remorse don't usually stop drinking or improve self-control, so get out now since waiting just makes it harder to leave and increases the risk that both of you will do something you'll regret. As long as you can protect yourself and your partner from uncontrolled abuse, take pride in your efforts. Most relationships sometimes require work to tolerate and keep from getting nasty; so as long as you meet those goals, be proud.

The longer a relationship lasts, the more it develops its own chemistry, which is seldom entirely positive or easy to live with. Do your best to straighten out misunderstandings, but be prepared to accept negative feelings and weaknesses as facts and decide whether the entire package is worthwhile.

At that point, it's time to decide what will work best in the long run, knowing that pain, whatever is decided, is unavoidable. It's simply the price of passionate chemistry, no matter what is the object—athletic, edible, anthropoid—of your intense affection.

## Sparking or Psycho?

It's unfortunate that exciting people are so quick to arouse us emotionally, not just because those emotions are often false or empty, but because, in the world of chemistry, exciting people are often like uranium: unstable, highly toxic, and possibly world-ending.

For reasons that defy common sense, Darwin, and our own self-interest, none are easier to vibe with than the kinds of people you want to avoid the most, e.g., those who are crazy, psychopathic, or just Assholes (see p. 77). Here are some common red flags in flirting that are too often mistaken for checkered.

| Sparking | Psycho | Why So? |
|---|---|---|
| She's into you from the moment you meet and unafraid to let you know (and have sex with you on the bus). | She will be not into you just as suddenly and be equally unafraid of the legal consequences of castrating you. | Technically speaking, she's got borderline personality disorder, which in not-technical terms is "crazy." Don't mistake intense excitement for an actual connection. |
| She trusts you implicitly, made more remarkable by the way she's been hurt before. | As you listen to her share her pain, you will go from being her boyfriend to being her full-time therapist or ER nurse. | We're often drawn to those who need rescuing, but it's better to pick up wounded animals at ASPCA shelters, not bars. |
| He makes you laugh, feel sexy, and generally happier than you can remember being. | He distracts you from realizing you know nothing about him or what he's capable of. | Anyone that focused on making you feel good wants something, and it isn't a stable relationship. |

| Sparking | Psycho | Why So? |
|---|---|---|
| He's not afraid to take a stand against injustice and tell you who the real Assholes are. | He thinks everyone is an Asshole who ever frustrated him, hurt his feelings, or maybe just made eye contact with him, and you know you could be next. | The intense emotionality of Assholes is attractive, but they can't have a bad feeling without blaming it on someone, and that someone will eventually be you. |
| He's fiercely protective of you, willing to stand up to and speak against anyone who's ever hurt you in the past, even if it's just the guy at the Taco Bell drive-through who only gave you one packet of hot sauce. | He goes from protective to paranoid, hating the people you hate while insisting that you actually like them more than you like him. Now all that anger is aimed at you, and there's no one to protect you anymore. | While most Assholes abuse those they consider enemies, others go after the ones they love. If he asks for your number, ask for a restraining order. |

## Marriage and Chemistry

A major goal of marriage, aside from not getting divorced, is creating something new, investing in it, and making something bigger than what you could have on your own (all of which gets torn apart, often fifty-fifty, if you can't make it work). So, as your marital chemistry changes due to stress from mutual responsibilities and all the things that can and do go wrong, remember that it's not just your happiness but your investment—emotional, financial, and otherwise—that's on the line.

Here are three examples:

- *I don't think I'm in love with my wife anymore. . . . Yes, I love her, but I don't know if that's enough. After ten years of marriage, the spark is gone; we seem more like roommates than lovers, more friendly than passionate. I find myself looking at other women, but I don't want to hurt her or break up our home. My goal is to get the spark back, one way or the other.*

- *I love my wife, as long as she's not drinking, but when she's drunk, she's just not the same person. Sure, we'd go out when we first met—we sort of fell in love during those fun nights, being stupid and young. She's not drinking for fun now, but at home to get wasted, and she's doing it a little too often. If I let her know how I feel, she just drinks more and tells me I'm destroying what little confidence she has. I think we've got a great marriage, but I'm not sure it can withstand this. My goal is to get her to do something about her drinking.*

- *My husband and I are lucky in that we have a loving relationship that is as strong now as when we first met; we have fun together, we're still attracted to each other, and if we're out alone, we're sometimes still mistaken for newlyweds. We were surprised, however, when our younger daughter's teacher said she thought our daughter was underperforming and maybe needed more attention. I admit, it's hard to take more time to help her with her homework without taking time away from my husband. My goal is to figure out how to make this happen or whether it's good advice.*

As hard as it is to find the right someone with the right chemistry, it's harder still to find a way to keep good chemistry intact during a marriage. That's because it's under endless attack by all the major uncontrollable forces in life, such as work, raising a family, and aging. If you're really lucky, your chemistry will evolve in perfect harmony with your relationship. If you've got average luck, you'll tolerate each other enough to avoid murder or suicide, or at least divorce.

So, as much as you'd like to have a relationship that grows stronger and happier over the years, you must often accept unavoidable conflicts and weaknesses that impose compromise and require painful decisions.

If your relationship becomes boring, trying to make it more interesting may do nothing but increase your longing for excitement; you're trying to turn your marriage back into a courtship, and since courtship is always temporary, your fix will be just as fleeting. You're wiser to accept the loss of excitement and decide what you want to do with it. Begin by appraising the value of your relationship and what it allows you to do.

If, for instance, your marriage gives you security, friendship, and help in creating and raising a family, you may well decide that excitement is unimportant and not particularly desirable. What's important is that you know what, in addition to excitement, matters to you and to make your decision on that basis. Remember, the only way to find true excitement in the same situation every day for several years is to either get a job in the stunt-driver industry or to become a goldfish. The more familiar something becomes, the more boring it gets, and as you age, this applies more and more; this can either feel comforting or depressing and terrifying.

Beware becoming the clichéd middle-aged/older man who flees his mortality straight into the doors of a hair-plugs clinic and out into the backseat of a sports car where there awaits a much younger woman who somehow makes a living via Craigslist. Assess whether it's your marriage that's stagnating or just your courage, and whether it's worth raging against your mortality instead of being grateful you have a steady partner to age alongside.

Addiction and other illnesses often change the chemistry of a relationship in ways that appear perfectly controllable. Unfortunately, addictive behaviors are anything but, and you may find it impossible to avoid facing that your once-fun companion now sometimes strikes you as embarrassing, aggressive, or unhelpful, and you find yourself struggling with feelings of loss and resentment.

Attacking addiction often backfires, though it's hard not to feel as if you have a right to complain and insist on treatment. After you discover the limits of complaining and insisting, encourage your spouse to weigh the differences that drinking has brought to her life and, if she sees what you see, to stop and seek help if she decides she needs it. But knowing that her wish to feel good, or at least not to feel bad, may be stronger than her desire to do what's good for her, add up your reasons for staying with her or letting go. Your job is not to blame her for ruining your life, but to accept that she's an addict and then decide what you (not she) can do about it.

Whether or not you decide to live with her alcoholism, don't accept the feeling that it controls you or your fate. Life is hard, compromise is necessary, and you should take pride in whatever compromises you decide to make.

Even long-lasting marital bliss can cause problems during a family's lifetime. Good for you if you're able to sustain a high level of happiness, but happiness is not the only reason that you married, and raising kids often requires periods of sacrifice and unhappiness. In fact, romantic happiness can often distract you from your parenting duties; it's the Ron and Nancy Reagan model of marital time management.

You must decide for yourself whether your child's needs require more of your time and energy. Just because your child has a problem doesn't mean that you have the answer or that you can't get good help from other sources; as a parent, you decide what's necessary. If, however, meeting your child's needs (according to your own standards) interferes with your extremely lovey-dovey marriage, then you must decide what's more important. It may not be a happy decision, but you can always be proud of making it in a way that reflects your values.

Interpersonal chemistry is a powerful force in every marriage. Whether it pushes you to stay or leave, don't expect it to let up, go away, or respond to your wishes. Instead, accept your feelings without letting them control your decisions.

Remember to value your marriage for all that it brings to your life and not just the way it makes you feel. If you can learn to accept the new rules and limits that come with life's changes, your chemistry may just evolve and survive.

## Did You Know . . . Truth, or Bullshit?

*We examine widely accepted beliefs about relationships to determine whether they're true (or not so much). The phrase in question:*
"We all fall for assholes every once in a while."

"Asshole" (capital *A*) is a clinical term; an Asshole is someone who believes he's the one honest person in a world gone mad, and it's his sacred duty to take arms against anyone who blocks his path to righteousness. For many of those people who've unwittingly stood in his path, their first stop postwrath is a shrink's office, which is why Assholes got a whole chapter in our last book.

Assholes are worth mentioning again here because, despite their name, they are strangely, dangerously attractive. If energy and excitement are the matches and lighter fluid of chemistry, it shouldn't be surprising that Assholes are alluring, given how passionate they are, and how compelling that passion can be (when it's not entirely directed toward your destruction).

> The strongly dramatic emotion their personality emits is like an animal musk; it may spell bad, but it also compels attention. Dogs may be powerless not to take a sniff, but as humans, we should know better.
>
> VERDICT: ALL TOO TRUE

There's no point in having a relationship without chemistry, but there are many valid reasons for avoiding a relationship with chemistry, such as when it's with a jerk, makes you forget your values, or has no hope for improvement. So your goal isn't to find good chemistry or find a way to make bad chemistry good; it's to know the chemistry you attract and generate, beware its weaknesses and dangers, and use it to fashion a good partnership that helps you be a good person with just enough good vibes to keep things intact.

| What to Look For | What to Achieve/What Not to Be Fooled By |
|---|---|
| Mutual attraction | . . . based on chemistry as well as personality and intelligence, not intense lust, loneliness, mania, hate, or a need to fill the vacuum left by the last loser you wasted three weeks with. |
| Mutual respect | . . . for work ethic and a good heart, not the good/ sexy vibes generated between the two of you. |
| Shared effort | . . . when you have tough things to do together and you're both tired and starting to hate each other, and not when you are getting each other off in exciting new ways (and boring old ones). |
| Common interests | . . . especially when it comes to your morals and vision for your family, not just looking into the bottomless pools of each other's eyes. |
| Common goals | . . . such as having kids, buying a house, and keeping those kids from getting their fingers pierced, and not riding your mutual buzz to a quick pregnancy that's meant to be a celebration of your intense love without any thought given to the kid's future. |

# Should I Go on a Date with This Person I'm Interested In?

Meeting people isn't hard—just ask people who push skin products at mall kiosks, any woman who's ever walked past lunching construction workers, or Craig Newmark. The hard part is meeting people you actually want to be around, let alone spend lots of time with, let alone spend naked time with that you won't regret soon afterward. Because it's so hard to find quality relationship candidates, people often leap into dating someone without looking too closely (at anything beyond their profile pic). While that's a quick fix to loneliness, it can be damaging in the long term; dating losers for immediate gratification can leave you jaded, exhausted, and derailed from the focus and time it takes to find someone worthwhile. So, before you pursue a could-be special someone, follow this chart to see whether he or she is worth it or not. If the chart says no, remember that accepting bad news from a book is easier than accepting a bad breakup that could have been avoided.

# Should I Go on a Date with This Person I'm Interested In?

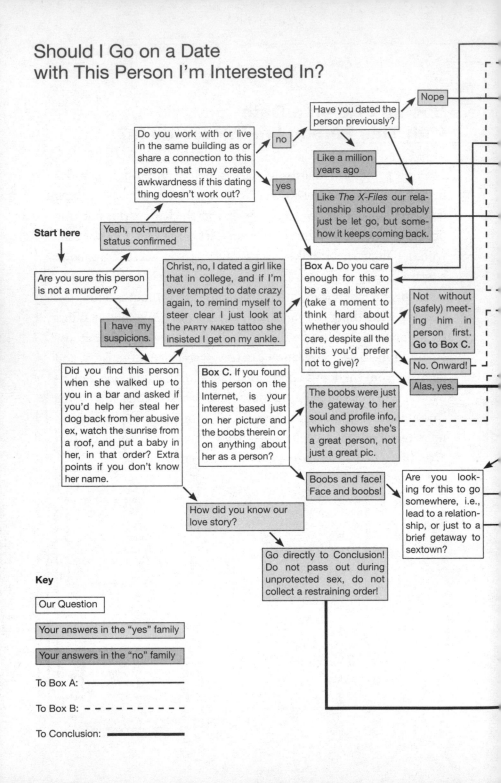

Nope

Have you dated the person previously?

Do you work with or live in the same building as or share a connection to this person that may create awkwardness if this dating thing doesn't work out?

no

yes

Like a million years ago

Like *The X-Files* our relationship should probably just be let go, but somehow it keeps coming back.

**Start here**

Yeah, not-murderer status confirmed

Are you sure this person is not a murderer?

Christ, no, I dated a girl like that in college, and if I'm ever tempted to date crazy again, to remind myself to steer clear I just look at the PARTY NAKED tattoo she insisted I get on my ankle.

**Box A.** Do you care enough for this to be a deal breaker (take a moment to think hard about whether you should care, despite all the shits you'd prefer not to give)?

Not without (safely) meeting him in person first. **Go to Box C.**

I have my suspicions.

No. Onward!

Alas, yes.

Did you find this person when she walked up to you in a bar and asked if you'd help her steal her dog back from her abusive ex, watch the sunrise from a roof, and put a baby in her, in that order? Extra points if you don't know her name.

**Box C.** If you found this person on the Internet, is your interest based just on her picture and the boobs therein or on anything about her as a person?

The boobs were just the gateway to her soul and profile info, which shows she's a great person, not just a great pic.

Boobs and face! Face and boobs!

Are you looking for this to go somewhere, i.e., lead to a relationship, or just to a brief getaway to sextown?

How did you know our love story?

Go directly to Conclusion! Do not pass out during unprotected sex, do not collect a restraining order!

**Key**

Our Question

Your answers in the "yes" family

Your answers in the "no" family

To Box A: ─────────

To Box B: ─ ─ ─ ─ ─ ─ ─ ─

To Conclusion: ▬▬▬▬▬▬▬

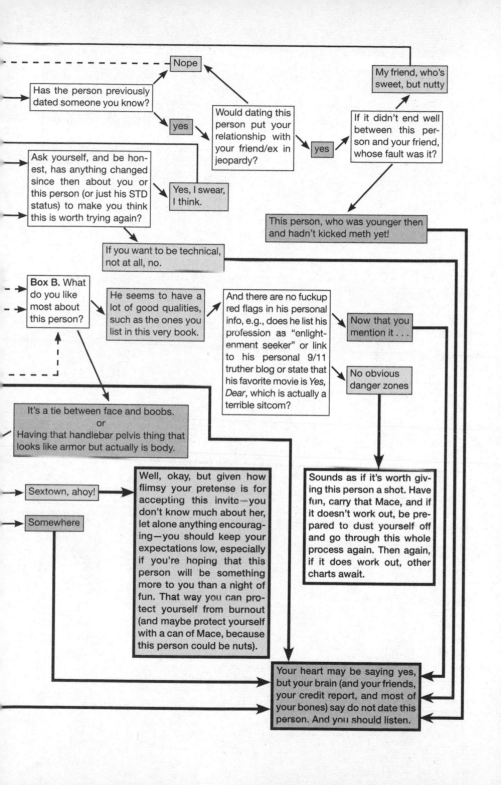

# Chapter 4

# F*ck Communication

The ability to talk, share, and understand one another has become one of the cornerstones of modern life; we can now communicate via email, text, tweet, status update, vicious-comment section, and stadium JumboTron. What this surge in communication should teach us, however, is that as valuable as talk can be in any context and via any medium, it can also be just as cheap.

In the world of relationships, good communication is considered a crucial element to making any union last, but "good" doesn't necessarily mean plentiful, constant, or even satisfying. It's important to learn to spot the dark side of close communication in relationships so you can protect yourself from overvaluing deep conversation or allowing it to drive partnership decisions off course.

It's easy to fool yourself into thinking that someone who is wonderful to talk to is, indeed, your new best friend and soul mate with whom you have found a unique shared language. Unfortunately, that person may just be a wonderful talker who speaks the universal language of bullshit. It's also easy to believe good communication can resolve conflicts and save you from ever having to go to bed angry, when, in actuality, the best kind of communication for certain conflicts is silence.

Like most dark sides, this kind of connection is inviting because it feels good, particularly if you're lonely, feel misunderstood, or are experiencing the mental pain of being on your own. Plus, it's supposed to be good for you, since good talk is what therapists (and other help-oriented professionals) are supposed to use as a means of improving your mental health. But even when the professional isn't exploitative or selfish, communication is not necessarily good for you or the long-term relationship you wish to build.

Aside from knowing that anything that feels good isn't necessarily good for you, you should also be able to recognize that this is especially true in the search for relationships; when you're looking for a partner, feeling good distracts you from doing smart detective work and spotting the red flags that ultimately lead to very bad feelings indeed (and possibly the need to hire a lawyer). So, without denying yourself the pleasures of good communication, don't forget that you have a job to do and facts to check.

As a relationship progresses, good communication seems to open the door to deeper intimacy, particularly if you're sharing thoughts and feelings you don't normally share with anyone else. If your standard for a special relationship is that it helps you discover who you are and overcome conventions that prevent you from being yourself, then rare and unusual communication seems meaningful. Just because a relationship is special or helps you grow, however, doesn't mean that it's supposed to last or that a stimulating friend is a solid partner.

If you get close by sharing words about hurt feelings or well-hated mutual enemies, you may experience rapid intimacy, but at a cost, not just to your relationship, but to yourself. Talking about

common enemies can be satisfying, but it does not necessarily form the foundation for a stable relationship or help you to see yourself as anyone other than a victim. Plus, people who are particularly aware of, and communicative about, negative feelings in general often wind up with negative feelings about you that they are quick to share with others. An awareness of feelings and an honest ability to share them, whether they're open and positive or private and malicious, is not a guarantee of perspective or integrity.

So beware the pleasure of easy, free communication. Don't let the satisfaction of feeling understood or the thrills of intimate gossip mislead you into neglecting your usual procedures for judging character, assessing behavior, and looking for a good match with someone whose talk is worthwhile.

## The Good Things You Want Communication to Deliver

- A sense of pleasurable anticipation when you start to talk and the secrets begin to flow.
- A feeling of confidence in your ability to say anything and be understood and not judged, no matter how evil or gross or stupid the contents of your mind.
- A unique intimacy that causes you to forget your inhibitions and somehow makes your sexual attraction yet sexier.
- A feeling of comfort and trust that could only come from finding the one person who understands you better than you do yourself (and may accept you and your private thoughts more than you do).
- A belief that your superior ability to communicate with your special someone will eliminate misunderstanding and solve all conflict between the two of you forever and, if you can extend your power, beget world peace.

## Profile of the Talented Talker

Here is a list of traits associated with someone with advanced communication skills:

- *Physical attributes:* Mobile facial expressions and active eye contact, often mirroring your own movements so as to better convey interest and intimacy, even if you're not in the same room and just communicating via emoji (she's *that good*).
- *Common occupations:* Those that require the ability to deftly convey ideas to an audience while making them feel listened to and understood, even if they never get a chance to speak (and aren't listened to when they do); e.g., advertising executive, politician, hairstylist, teacher, and of course therapist.
- *What attracts you first:* The rush that comes with finding someone you can share your secrets with, and then getting to admit those secrets, and then getting to hear her secrets (or just fake secrets she makes up for the illusion of intimacy).
- *Red flags:* You know way too much about her way too soon, not just information you might not be ready to hear, but details you aren't interested in and pet peeves and rants that are decidedly unattractive. Never mind the stories of being victimized and betrayed by once-trusted friends, which are making you wonder whether this gal is just terrible at picking friends or terrible at keeping them.

## Seeking Communication

It's natural to identify new friends and good dates by their ability to communicate easily and spontaneously, even if it's initially about topics provided by a dating service or displayed via a particularly

insightful photo you can't not swipe right on. After all, if communicating requires too much work, it's a sign that you're not on the same wavelength. Some people, however, are still good, smart relationship candidates, despite not being good talkers, because they communicate less with words and more by deeds, laughter, and facial expression. Other candidates are good talkers (or picture posers), but they use their communication skills to mask their shortcomings. Your job is to persist in determining what communication means and whether it reflects the qualities you're looking for in a long-lasting relationship with a person you can trust.

Here are three examples:

- *My new boyfriend is great at telling me how he feels and being a good ear, and it's so nice to finally be with someone who asks me about my day and genuinely cares about my answer. Basically, there's no one I trust more, so I didn't hesitate to lend him money he needed to get a new TV (his credit is maxed out from making a bunch of do-or-die student loan payments). Yet sometimes I feel jealous when he's paying close attention to someone else, and sometimes I feel insecure about whether our relationship is his priority. My goal is to get over my insecurity and not let suspicion and jealousy get in the way of trust.*

- *For the past few months, I've been dating the sweetest, most sensitive, generous man I've ever met. He's always there for me when I need his time, ear, and support. The only problem is that, sometimes, he goes off for weeks at a time to take care of his sister and her kids because she's a drug addict who relies on him even more than I do (but is a lot less trustworthy and takes from him without giving anything in return). When I try to confront him about how much she abuses his generosity and empathy, he just*

*shuts down, and the whole sister situation is what's preventing us
from getting serious together. My goal is to figure out how to show
him that, if he wants a life with me, he has to let his sister figure
out her life on her own.*

- *I've had a couple boyfriends who were nice, reliable, and
genuinely interested in me, but they couldn't talk about feelings or
do much besides grunt if their lives depended on it. Spending time
with them always left me feeling lonely and in need of a good, long
talk with my best friend. My goal is to find someone who likes to
talk about the things I'm interested in, isn't gay, and could be my
best friend.*

If starting conversations with attractive people you don't know
feels like tense, sweaty, mortifying torture, as it does for so many
people, then nothing seems more valuable in courting than the
ability to get a conversation going. Whether that ability is yours or
belongs to the person you're dying to get to know, carrying on a
conversation until you're able to calm down and feel comfortable
is the best way to ease the torture while also getting closer to the
source of your excitement.

It seems logical to define a good first date by the ease with which
you talked and the ability of your conversation to distract you from
everything else, particularly the time, your flop sweat, his breath,
etc. However, good communication, beyond the first meeting, can
be as dangerous and complicated as it is pleasurable.

Since trust is such a warm and welcome feeling, it's tempting to
want to act on it right away and, if you have lingering suspicions,
ignore them for fear of ruining a romance. With a good communicator, those suspicions are often built-in, because if he can gain
your trust and make you feel special so quickly, you can't help but

worry that he's just as able to connect with others and make them feel special, too. If you start to criticize yourself for feeling needy or insecure, however, you're forgetting that it's your job to worry and withhold trust until you figure out whether you do, indeed, have a special relationship or whether you're just being charmed into giving up your time, body, and hard-earned cash.

It's smart, not paranoid, as someone who's lent this person money and has a stake in his finances, to find out more about the way he manages it. You're entitled to know whether he has credit-card debt and how he deals with student loans, savings, and other outstanding debts. You also need to know how he plans to pay you back and how well he's been able to repay previous loans.

Don't test his integrity by expressing negative feelings and watching how he responds because you'll be asking for possibly empty reassuring words. What you want to see is genuine reliable behavior, so instead of soliciting contrite promises, carefully watch his actions, such as whether he makes time for you two to be together, how well he tolerates your bad moods when good communication just isn't possible, and, most important, whether he follows through on promises, such as the one to pay you back.

If he says he's hurt that you don't trust him and feels that your questions have damaged a budding romance, don't accept his definition of mistrust or a good relationship. You're as positive about the relationship as he is, but he has brought up his need for money, so your finding out how he manages money is necessary to protect your relationship from the bad feelings that always arise from misunderstandings about loans. Instead of blaming yourself for trying to get to know more about a guy who seems unusually trustworthy, give yourself credit for your ability to put aside your need for closeness until you've gathered enough facts to be sure that a good communicator is, indeed, someone you can trust.

Other good talkers who are also superior listeners are more likely
to be taken advantage of than vice versa; they aren't evil communicators, but overextended ones. When someone is ultraresponsive
to your needs, you may find that he's passive and makes you too
responsible for his life decisions. He may be agreeable for long periods of time and then suddenly complain of feeling dominated and
controlled. Or, as you've experienced, he may be a slave to his whiniest family member or coworker and become responsive to you only
when you blow up and try to snatch the title of whiniest for yourself.

So trust your instincts and look for evidence of independent-
mindedness, even when it interferes with pleasant communication.
Find out if your no-boundaries boyfriend can ever learn to say no
to his sister by asking him if his taking responsibility for her welfare
is helping her in the long run. Yes, helping her may make him feel
useful or guilt relieved. It's probable, however, that she's asking him
to do for her many things she should be doing for herself, and that
his helpfulness is encouraging bad behavior and discouraging her
from ever becoming healthier or independent.

Urge him to raise this issue with a professional counselor; you
hope that you're wrong, but, if you're right, working with a counselor will make him more helpful while also giving him more control over his own time. Being truly helpful is not a matter of feeling
helpful, it's a matter of doing the right thing.

Describe your having a possible relationship with each other as
something that could help both of you start a new life. If he can't
free up enough time and effort, he won't be able to build a partnership with anyone, and that would be sad. What you want to see is
whether he can sustain a commitment to his own future; if he can't,
then you shouldn't, either.

Rating undercommunicators is difficult because it's not fun,
takes time, and is basically everything an intimate conversation

is not. Shyness may interfere with communication when you first meet someone, so give yourself enough time to see if he opens up after he knows you better. It's also wise to find ways of communicating that don't depend entirely on words, such as activities that require teamwork or some kind of give-and-take (going on a road trip, programming a DVR, surviving an afternoon at IKEA, etc.).

If you're not overly dependent on gabby partners (and are happy to outsource your communication needs to friends, hairstylists, or cats), are properly respectful of other ways guys can share and contribute, and still know your minimum limit for verbal communication, then respect your own standards and see if he has what it takes. Observe his ability to express himself at work or with old friends, or ask for his thoughts on topics that should be safe and easy. Then ask yourself whether his nonverbal warmth and handyman contributions are enough to make you happy.

Don't let the lubricating quality of easy conversation ease you into an otherwise rough relationship; stick with your basic system for rating character and compatibility, regardless of whether someone is delightful to talk to or hates to open his mouth. Even if talking is like pulling teeth, don't write him off until you've taken time to do an objective evaluation. Relationships may begin with conversation, but they live and die by character and behavior.

*Quiz: Communication Questionnaire—Is this good line of communication also a good relationship starter?*

1. You've been having such a good conversation with the pretty girl at the bar that you didn't even notice that hours have gone by and everyone else has left and gone home. To best wrap up this magical evening, you would:

    A: Tell her, frankly, that you have to see her again because you

feel you can tell her everything, like, say, that you were sui-
cidal earlier this month and meeting her has given you new
hope.

B:  Tell her you've got work tomorrow and should go anyway but
that maybe you'll see her again at this same bar sometime
(attempting to make more specific plans would just lead to
awkwardness and rejection).

C:  Get her phone number, offer to help her get a cab or walk her
home, and tell her how much you've enjoyed talking to her.

2.  You've always been shy and wary about office romance, but the
woman working in the next cubicle laughs at your jokes and likes
the same movies, and you find yourself looking forward to your
chats by the water cooler. You decide to:

A:  Ask her out because she's such a great person to talk to, even
though the last time you dated someone from work she
ended up talking to all your coworkers *about* you after you
broke up and it was a year before your coworkers stopped
looking at your crotch.

B:  Avoid a potential disaster by bringing your own water to
work and avoiding her completely.

C:  Invite her to have lunch with you and your other work friends
and get to know her very, very slowly.

3.  Your new boyfriend is easy to talk to and you text each other so
constantly that you've burned through your data plan and your
chin has fused to your chest. If you didn't hear from him for two
days, you would:

A:  Call a SWAT team because the only reason he'd go silent like
that is if he was being held hostage at gunpoint by the Sym-
bionese Liberation Army.

B: Keep radio silence until he tries to reach you a couple times, then stay cool and detached so he knows you're fine without him and you can avoid any sort of confrontation.

C: Text him about what you're doing and ask if he's okay, hope he responds, then distract yourself with work, the Internet, yoga, etc., to best resist the urge to check in again.

4. Your boyfriend shares everything with you, and you feel there's nothing you can't talk about, but you notice he drinks a lot on weekends and doesn't always allow other people to drive him home from the bar. You decide to:

A: Tell him frankly that he's driving you crazy with worry and you can't stand to see him drink and put himself in danger (right before his mother reads a similar statement, since you've arranged an intervention).

B: Send him a link to a particularly gruesome article about a DUI accident and, if he doesn't respond then, just stop talking to him from Friday through Monday (or start on Thursday afternoon, just to be safe).

C: Tell him you've noticed this pattern on weekends and ask him what his standards are for safe drinking and whether he thinks he's meeting those standards.

5. You and your girlfriend don't always agree, but you both hate the people who live in the apartment next door, and angrily ranting about them always sparks good jokes and brings you together. One day, when they're having a loud fight, you decide to:

A: Knock on their door together, go full good cop/bad cop, and warn them that you'll call the real police if they don't stop. Then spend the next week happily/angrily recalling the event to each other so loudly that the neighbors call the cops on *you*.

B:  Move. To another state. And change your name.

C:  Ask your landlord to intervene without mentioning your
    names. In the meantime, purchase noise-canceling head-
    phones and look at apartment listings.

If you answered mostly A's . . .

You're an oversharer who doesn't stop to think about where
expressing your feelings is likely to lead; even when it initially
makes you feel closer to someone you care about, it could eventually put you in an awkward, or even dangerous, position. Remind
yourself that it's not good to get too close to someone who doesn't
know you, might not be sticking around, or likes jumping into
conflicts you should avoid.

If you answered mostly B's . . .

Your fears of conflict or rejection prevent you from identifying
problems, proposing solutions, and letting people know where
you stand. You avoid confrontation and opening up at all costs,
which means you keep yourself too far removed from the people
around you. Keep your wariness, but learn to test out your fears,
because if you can barely share your space or your thoughts with
others, you certainly can't share your life with one of them.

If you answered mostly C's . . .

You like getting closer, but you see the risks as well as the benefits. You take time to gather facts, observe closely, and check
out whether there are any deal breakers (or the traits of possible
serial killers). You've mastered the art of getting close while keeping a safe distance.

## Simple Tips for the Silent Type

If you're not a big talker, here's the little that's required of you communication-wise.

- If she looks upset, don't put off asking "What's wrong?"—the longer you wait, the louder/more visual her answer will be when asking becomes unavoidable.
- Tell her she looks nice, because if you tell her frequently enough, she'll stop asking.
- Remember, *death before sulking*, so if you're upset, suck it up until you figure out whether it's a big deal and then develop a positive way to talk about it.
- When you don't have anything funny, interesting, or insightful to say, don't just respond with a monosyllabic answer or a wet grunt; ask her questions and she'll appreciate your interest and keep finding funny, interesting, or insightful stuff to tell *you*.
- Tell her what you've done to fix up the place or car or toilet and ask her opinion about how to possibly make it better—even if she doesn't know how, at least it's a topic you're comfortable getting into (except for maybe details about the toilet).

## Having Good Communication

Having the gift of gab can be a huge part of having game, period. Knowing you're good at communicating with the opposite sex can give you confidence in your ability to find a partner and keep her interested. Your confidence may, however, mislead you into saying whatever you feel like without thinking about the power of words to create attachment, mutual dependence, and even fear if you plow through boundaries before one or both of you is ready. Don't let your gift for good talk create close connections before you've assessed the risks and decided they're not a bad bet.

Here are three examples:

- *I know I'm not such a handsome guy, but I've always found it easy to talk to girls in bars and establish a natural connection that leads easily to hooking up without the conversation getting too serious or implying anything permanent. Even though these girls are cool with not having a serious romantic relationship, that we connect so strongly through talk often leads them to expect a lasting friendship that is deeper than I want, with regular communication and close mutual support. I like to go my own way, period, no matter how I got into their pants. My goal is to enjoy the intimacy without creating false expectations.*

- *I'm good at communicating what I'm feeling—I believe that it's probably damaging to bottle things up and hold back when you have something to say—and it's led to some good, close relationships, but then things always seem to go wrong. At some point, even my closest friends seem to misinterpret what I'm saying or they ignore it and respond as if I were criticizing them, or asking for something unfair, or just being inappropriate and "nuts." My goal is to find out where my communication is failing so I can take close relationships to a higher level.*

- *I've always had a gift for friendship and can talk to almost anyone and make people laugh and feel comfortable expressing themselves, but it's hard to get guys to see me as more than an ear. They love to talk to me, particularly when they're unhappy about something, but instead of that leading to serious dating, I find myself stuck in friend purgatory (and not the acceptable kind with nights out and occasional awkward hookups, but the kind where I become their ad hoc crisis counselor, prized for my advice-giving over fun-having). My goal is to figure out how to make my communication skills lead to partnership rather than second-banana friendship.*

While good communication skills may give you the power to start and deepen the bonds of relationships, they do not negate the underlying needs that bring people together and determine how or whether they will get along. In the proverbial body of a relationship, communication is merely the circulatory system, while those underlying needs and values are the skeleton, and without a complete set of bones, you aren't going to last long or go far.

For instance, if you see communication as a means to a sexual end and your partners see it as the end achieved by sexual means, they may well grow disappointed with what they regard as your relative unavailability and feel that your friendliness promises more than it delivers. Your relationship doesn't resemble a body so much as a grotesque blob.

No laws of social commerce oblige you to meet your sexual partners' social needs when they are stronger than your own and were never part of the sexual arrangement to begin with. If, however, you try to explain, after the fact, that you have affection and respect but no great desire to spend nonbedroom time together, you may wind up deepening rather than easing the hurt. Instead, put yourself in their shoes and ask yourself how much clarification and advanced warning you would like to receive from someone who was genuinely friendly but did not wish to be more than a casual friend in the long run.

You have a duty to protect yourself from exploitation, but you may also decide that a good person should impose fair disclosure rules on him- or herself so as not to inadvertently exploit others. So instead of letting charm and sexual needs dictate your actions, confirm that your partners are no more interested in social relationships than you are and be more specific about where you stand. You don't have to reject anyone personally to let her know that, as much as you enjoy her company, your social interest in her (and probably others) is relatively limited. As a result of such selectivity, you may have fewer sexual encounters, but the ones you do have will be on mutually agreed terms with women with whom you share both a desire and a desired level of commitment, and be more enjoyable in the long run.

Having good communication with someone can also cause trouble if you don't know when to shut your mouth. Even when a relationship makes you feel as if you can talk about anything and everything, you will always discover some issues and beliefs that can cause hurt and misunderstanding. If you assume that good communication can always establish rapport and remove disagreements, you may try harder to discuss these topics and so make misunderstandings worse. Instead, respect that communication is a gift and blessing that can also enhance the risk of conflict.

Don't let neediness or the pleasures of a gabfest cause you to share too much too quickly, or to share too much in general. Be cautious while watching carefully for signs that your words are being misunderstood, and if you find a disturbing difference in basic assumptions and beliefs, don't assume that it results from a misunderstanding that additional words will clear up.

Instead of pressing your point of view or sharing your feelings, try to understand where the difference comes from and whether its roots are deep; yes, it's less fun and spontaneous when you have to be careful about what you say in a close relationship, but having basic differences does not make a close relationship impossible, just less easy. The spontaneity of your communication gives you a gift for intimacy, but also makes it easier for your mouth to get you into trouble. Learning to be a little less spontaneous and unfiltered won't destroy your talent for getting close, and once you are close, it will greatly improve your ability to stay that way.

Just as you can't control the fundamental differences your communication skills uncover in a relationship, you also can't control other aspects of interpersonal chemistry, such as a lack of sexual attraction or romantic interest. As a result, you may find yourself spending a lot of time getting emotionally intimate with people with whom physical intimacy isn't in the cards.

It's worth asking your close friends whether you're doing something wrong, perhaps by acting too much like a good buddy with a good ear to those who are nowhere near as interested in hearing about who you are and when you're available. It's possible, however, that you're doing nothing wrong, and that your personality simply attracts a kind of relationship that is not special or partnership oriented.

Let your partnership needs determine your priorities. Don't feel responsible for returning friendly overtures simply because someone needs to talk, you like him, and you enjoy hanging out; if you don't need friends, save your efforts until you find someone with whom friendliness seems more personal and partnership directed. Yes, you may find yourself lonely and with time on your hands, but you'll need an open schedule if you're to be ready for the right person when he comes along.

Never assume that a gift for communication makes relationships easy beyond the initial stage. If you learn how to manage your gift in the context of your values and experience, you can use it to start and enhance a worthwhile relationship with strong bones and a healthy heart.

## The Art of Apology: The Dos and Don'ts of Sorry

The words "I love you" are hardly as difficult to say as some people think. "I'm sorry," on the other hand, when expressed sincerely in the wake of an acknowledged and indefensible error, doesn't just express a feeling but an entire thought process. Telling people you're sorry is letting them know that you've thought about what you've done, realized you've screwed up, want them to know you feel bad for screwing up, and, in taking the blame for screwing up, are less likely to screw up again. Even when "I love you" is sincere, it often just means that you want to go halfsies on a Hulu subscription.

Given the complex meaning of a good apology, it's not surprising that bad apologies are far too common. We're referring here not to the lamely delivered "I'm sorry," but to elaborate apologies that are built to deflect anger or blame, acceptance of which is the whole point of an apology. Worse, the blame is often placed on the person being apologized to, e.g., "I'm sorry you're such an idiot and are feeling so angry," which is less apology, more passive-aggressive bitch slap.

After a major fuckup, especially in a relationship, there's good reason to swallow your pride, admit your guilt, and accept your sentence. Here are some of the common nonapologies and their genuine/superior substitutes.

| Offense | Don't | Why? | Do |
|---|---|---|---|
| Said something inappropriate or offensive | I'm sorry you misinterpreted my words. | It's not his fault he was in earshot of your tactless ramblings and reacted to what seemed like their obvious meaning. | I realize what I said was offensive, and I'm sorry. I will try to be more thoughtful in the future. |

| Offense | Don't | Why? | Do |
|---|---|---|---|
| Done something thoughtless or stupid | I'm sorry I'm such an asshole. | Congratulations, you have now put the person you've hurt on the defensive, even though she probably never explicitly called you an asshole, just called you on fucking up (which you did, and need to apologize for). | I'm sorry I screwed up, it was a thoughtless mistake, and I have no good excuse for making it. It wasn't personal, but that doesn't mean I won't try to do better by you going forward. |
| Overheard making a nasty or mocking comment | I'm sorry I wasn't more discrete and careful about expressing myself. | You need to be sorry for being a dick, not sorry for being caught. | What I said was childish and unkind, and I'm not proud of my behavior. I'm sorry, and I hope to grow from this experience. |
| Caught in a lie | I'm sorry I didn't feel comfortable being honest with you. | You can blame an airline, in-law, tight shoe, etc., for making you uncomfortable, but you're the only one who chooses to be a liar. | I'm sorry I was dishonest, and I should have known better, but I took the easy way out. I'll find a way to be stronger and tell the truth from here on. |
| You make a dumb decision without consulting your partner | I'm sorry you can't appreciate that I made the right call. | . . . is the same as saying, "I'm not sorry that I don't give a shit what you think, dumbass." | I'm sorry I got swept up in what I feel strongly is the best solution. I shouldn't have acted without asking your opinion. I'll do better next time. |

## Communication and Marriage

One major fear people have about marriage is that one day they'll wake up next to someone with whom they have nothing to talk about; that they'll find that their spouse has become a stranger or, best-case scenario, an old, boring friend. But a marriage with easy and constant communication can be far more dangerous than a quiet monotonous one. While communication skills are, indeed, good for avoiding and removing misunderstanding and persuading your partner to do what you want him to, they may also convey negative feelings about problems and personal qualities that can't be changed. Knowing when not to communicate—whether it's while waking up, going to sleep (see sidebar on p. 106), or anything in between—is probably as important in preserving partnerships as communication is to getting them started.

Here are three examples:

- *My husband was on the fence about marriage, but I made a compelling case and talked him into marrying me because I loved him, knew he loved me, and thought it would be good for both of us. Five years in, however, he often acts as if he'd rather be free of marital obligations and out with his friends. I wonder if I overestimated what I and marriage have to offer him, and always feel like I'm failing to deliver the package I told him would make him happy and be worth it for both of us in the long run. My goal is to get him to talk about what he doesn't like in our marriage so I can either change it or get him to see that he's not being reasonable.*

- *When we started living together, my wife and I could tell each other absolutely everything—it was a major reason that I wanted to get married and knew we'd be happy together—but now that she's stressed by a child and a difficult job, she just takes our open communication as an opportunity to air constant criticism of everything I do, and it's driving me nuts. If I ask her to stop, she tells me that she has always valued mutual honesty and thinks it's important that she can speak frankly with me. My goal is to get her to see me more positively so that her communication becomes less critical.*

- *My wife always wonders why we don't talk anymore, but after two kids and ten years of sharing a bathroom, is there anything left unshared or unsaid? We get along well and work well together as parents, but once we've gone over our schedules and what we did at work, I'm out of topics. It's not like I resent her and share my thoughts with somebody else—if I were to "open up" to anyone, it would be her—but the conversation factory is basically closed. My goal is to get my wife to see that, just because there's not a lot to talk about, we don't have relationship problems and don't need to see a shrink.*

Since good communication is the key to diplomacy, it's not surprising that we expect good communicators to be able to apply the skills required to negotiate peace treaties, broker the release of hostages, or halt a nuclear apocalypse to solving the everyday conflicts of marriage. In actuality, however, it's probably easier for a diplomat to get two terrorist groups to join forces and start an organic farm than it is for a wife to will her husband into being more enthusiastic about their marriage. Failing to accept that sad reality can make any marital conflict that much worse.

If you're effective at persuasion, you may, for instance, be able to talk someone into marrying you. Once you've talked him into doing something he wouldn't otherwise have done, you're then responsible for all his marital unhappiness, which is impervious to your powers; the more you try to get him to spend time with you, the more unhappy he gets. Unfortunately, most things we might wish to change about our spouses are not responsive to persuasion, and trying it just increases the problem.

Once you accept the limits of your control, you can better help him understand his choices and encourage him to do whatever he thinks is best. For example, instead of trying to persuade him to be a more available partner, identify the amount of availability you think is reasonable and let him know where you stand. Say you want him around most evenings, minus the marital resentment. If he can't swing that bare minimum, you have a marriage that doesn't work for you and time's a-wasting to find an arrangement that does.

Let him know that, as much as you believe you two have the potential for a good marriage, commitment requires sacrifice and it won't work unless he wants marriage as much as you do. If he doesn't want it, make it clear that you will no longer try to persuade him to do anything; you'll simply move on and wish him well, knowing you've said what needed saying and the rest is up to him.

Communication for the sake of venting is similarly limited in its effectiveness and usually causes more pain than it promises to relieve. Encouraged, perhaps, by therapists and TV advisers, many people are confident shared feelings will lead to good conversation, and they will vent anger and hurt hoping to clear the air and relieve internal pressure. As we've said before, this logic may apply to intestinal gas, but the poison unleashed by releasing opinions will not dissipate so easily.

Unfortunately, communication has little influence over many sources of pain in a long-term partnership, including frustration with personality traits and certain behaviors that will never change, no matter how emphatically you state your displeasure, so airing feelings does nothing but start a fight and stoke lingering resentments.

Since the person who believes in communication regards the ensuing conflict as a problem requiring more communication, things often escalate until the couple seeks treatment at the ultimate "safe place," a therapist's office. Unfortunately, therapists, being mere mortals and not earthbound gods or enchanted lizard people, lack the power to stem the destructiveness of this process.

If you can't persuade your wife to rein in her determination to share, stop defending yourself or trying to change her mind. Instead, prepare a list of her standard criticisms and confirm with yourself that they have been properly aired and listened to in the past and should now be retired. If any haven't been addressed, by all means make an effort, but if you're sure there's no more you can do, then let her know, respectfully, that you believe communication about them should stop and that you will end further discussion, by withdrawing from it if necessary. You can't stop an overcommunicator from wanting to be overly honest, but you can reduce her airtime and incentive until talking is simply not worth it.

If, instead, peace and quiet have become boring to your partner and she complains that the silence between you is driving her crazy, don't expect good communication will talk her into believing that she should be happy. Yes, you may be doing many good things to contribute to your partnership, but as long as she feels talk deprived, her pain will only hurt more if you don't accept it. What you can do, after accepting her feelings as they are, is to let her know, without anger, that your silence doesn't reflect a lack of interest in her or your relationship. You're sorry that talking doesn't come easily to you, and you're interested in finding things to do that will bring you closer.

Then suggest activities that you would enjoy doing together and take time to express an interest in her opinions and feelings. Even if you can't think of interesting things to say, find ways to let her know that your relationship is always a top priority. You may well find that you can make her happier without having to change her needs or feelings or your own nonverbal style.

Good communication makes you feel that you can get close and overcome conflict whenever you want to, but if you can't appreciate its limits, you'll end up talking yourself into trouble and possibly divorce. Forget about learning the fine art of persuasion and brokering peace; instead, figure out how to use your common sense to tell you when it's time to talk, time to shut up, and time to find other ways to spend time together.

### Did You Know . . . Truth, or Bullshit?

*We examine widely accepted beliefs about relationships to determine whether they're true (or not so much). The phrase in question:*
"Never go to bed angry."

There's nothing wrong with not wanting to let a new day start with an ongoing conflict; that's why this phrase should instead be "Never start the day angry." Because it's much better to go to bed angry than to try to come up with a smart, peaceful, reasonable resolution to a contentious argument during the time of day you're least likely to be smart, peaceful, reasonable, or even cogent.

Bad fights often happen in the hours before bed because, shockingly, it's when most people are tired; at the end of a long day, people are often worn so thin that the slightest irritation sets them off. In the morning light, most of these disagreements are seen for what they are—meaningless, exhausted bickering—and naturally dissipate.

Even if these fights are the culmination of long-running disagreements, or if the fight takes place earlier but the resentment lingers until lights-out, the moments before going to sleep are not the ones when anyone's in the best shape for conflict resolution. Besides, last-minute fixes are rarely worthwhile, even when you come up with them when you're not half-awake.

So aim instead to sleep on it and talk about it in the morning (if there is in fact anything substantial to talk about after you've had a chance to rest and think it through). It's better to go to sleep mad than keep fighting for hours and barely get any sleep at all.

VERDICT: BULLSHIT

Communication is a gift that can help you get through to people, but it can't be used to make over people and undo the effects of bad character, bad chemistry, or bad behavior. Improve your communication skills if you can, but remember not to let interaction skills— your own or anyone else's—distract you from assessing a person's character and past actions as you look for what he or she can contribute to a partnership, not just communicate about it.

| What to Look For | What to Achieve/What Not to Be Fooled By |
| --- | --- |
| Mutual attraction | . . . from being able to hang out in the same room and enjoy each other's company without talking, rather than from being able to stare into each other's eyes and verbalize every thought with intense emotion. |
| Mutual respect | . . . because of what you know about the other person's work, character, and endurance when stressed and not based on your ability to entertain or vent every negative emotion to each other. |
| Shared effort | . . . that continues even when there's not much to say, rather than requiring you to chatter like the TV commentators at the Westminster Dog Show. |

| What to Look For | What to Achieve/What Not to Be Fooled By |
| --- | --- |
| Common interests | . . . in priorities arising from work, family, and individual interests, rather than knowing the contents of each other's minds, hearts, and spleens. |
| Common goals | . . . such as figuring out ways to best run a household, rather than learning how to express every last thought, desire, or food craving. |

# Five Ways to Prevent Yourself from Getting Worn-Out by Internet Dating

1. *Ask yourself what you want a relationship for:* There's nothing wrong with wanting someone for sex and socializing, but unless you're insensitive to rejection and personality mismatches, you'd better give priority to finding someone committed, supportive, and hardworking, not just somebody suitable for short-term sexy times. Otherwise, you'll wear yourself out with people you can't force yourself to care about or can't expect to hang around the moment you sound boring or stop looking good.

2. *Write up a job description for the position of life partner:* Yes, you have to hit it off and get along and fall in love et al., but only with someone who hits all the right marks on a checklist of required behavior. Since you need someone who can share social time, stick to commitments, and do her share while still taking care of her own shit, write up a job-listing-like description of the required duties, character qualities, and experience you require from a partner. In the absence of a romantic CV, look for those traits in her actions or in her relationship history. The more specific you are about the behavior you require, the more effectively you'll screen out candidates who may be attractive but don't have the credentials you need.

3. *Consider and list the assets you offer a partnership:* For this purpose, ignore superficial qualities, such as physical attractiveness and size of sneaker collection, and emphasize the Jane Austen–esque, bottom-line attributes such as financial security, honesty, and a willingness to work hard. Think of your assets in the same

way as you would those of a prospective partner; if you don't want to look for a life partner based on their fancy footwear, then putting your best metaphorical foot forward has more to do with who you are than what you have.

4. *Put it in writing:* Prepare a statement describing what you offer and what you're after, as well as a list of the questions you want answered. You don't need to read it to prospective dates verbatim, but you can't let a desire to appear attractive and chill get in the way of your laying things out, so prepare as you would before a job interview of someone you want to hire. The idea isn't to force you to ask intrusive questions instead of having a normal conversation, but to keep your mind on the information you're trying to gather and convey, tactfully, while not being distracted by other things. The more businesslike you are, the more effectively you'll screen out socializers and hookup artists.

5. *Don't meet with anyone you haven't vetted first:* Until you've done screening by email, text, phone, and/or second opinion, don't meet up and risk wasting your time. You can usually screen effectively for intelligence and sincerity if you don't try too hard to be funny and entertaining as you're doing it. Use a friend or a therapist as a coach to help you make contacts selective, brief, and efficient. If you see too many people for too long, you'll burn out. Don't meet until you've done good screening, and don't continue to meet if you encounter a red flag. Your job isn't to figure out why something isn't working, but to protect yourself and your time by quickly ditching bad dates and using the experience to choose better candidates next time and keep burnout at bay.

# Chapter 5

# F*ck a Sense of Humor

In most close relationships, be they friendships or romantic partnerships, the key moments that bond us are when we allow ourselves to be vulnerable together. That can mean helping each other through a painful rejection or illness, but it can also mean sharing a massive, pants-peeing laugh that is totally unfunny to everyone else.

Aside from the possibility of incontinence, being funny or amused might not seem like vulnerability, but cracking a joke or letting out a loud guffaw does require a bit of bravery, especially in front of someone you're attracted to (even if you don't have a strange sense of humor or a laugh that sounds like a donkey having an asthma attack). That's why humor always seems like a positive force for forming, finding, or sustaining relationships.

When people first meet, laughter is an especially effective tool for creating bonds; it makes us more attractive to each other while lowering barriers to talking and getting to know each other. It's the sign of a good beginning, and as a relationship progresses, the amount of laughter seems like a reliable measure of how well a relationship is doing.

After all, a shared sense of humor isn't just a sign of compatibility or of sharing a common point of view, but of being able to take pleasure in life's inconsistencies rather than turning them into rage and resentment. Humor implies a perspective that reduces competitiveness, anxiety, and hostility. It takes the edge off forces that make us wary, reactive, and ready to fight without thinking twice about what we're doing.

A high laughter quotient in a relationship indicates a strong ability to enjoy life and each other's company. It tends to spread and get other people to laugh and feel better. Laughter's even supposed to be good for your health. As positive human qualities go, a sense of humor can seem like fish oil, kale, and spin class combined.

There's no guarantee, however, that humor is always friendly or won't be used as a weapon to mock and belittle. Certain people who make us laugh are entertaining, but can be too sarcastic to relax with or welcome as friends. Humor sometimes can and should make us wary about potential relationships.

Even so, we seldom doubt our ability to recognize humor that is friendly, as well as clever, warm, and safe. Thus it draws us into new relationships and shapes our perception of old ones. It takes an effort, however, to remember that humor can be manufactured and is usually a form of communication, not a cure to all that ails you or a way to judge a person overall. Someone who can make you laugh isn't necessarily reliable or honest, just entertaining and able to make you feel good, which can distract you from your job of figuring out who a person really is. Just because someone has a good sense of humor doesn't mean he or she is a good partner, or even a good person.

So, as strong as the bonds formed by laughter can be, don't let them bind you to someone who's good for a laugh but terrible as a spouse. Don't let it distract you from getting to know people by their actions, not by their jokes, because as risky as it can be to be funny, humor's sometimes used to avoid the greater risk of showing one's true self.

## The Good Things You Want Humor to Deliver

- A pleasurable connection with someone who is entertaining and interested in entertaining you, as if you were living in your own private Branson, Missouri.
- An antidote to shyness, awkwardness, and wishing you were dead when you're trying to chat someone up.
- A sense of intimacy from finding you're annoyed by the same things and people and can laugh over your shared hatred and bitterness.
- A sense of closeness when you're feeling alienated, misunderstood, or shat on and laughed at.
- An answer to the anxiety of becoming vulnerable with someone you don't yet know that doesn't involve alcohol or being born-again.

## Profile of the Joker

Here is a list of traits associated with someone with a killer sense of humor:

- *Physical attributes:* While not necessarily covered in clown paint, a joker seems to relish looking unconventional, either by trying too hard (from Hawaiian shirt to wrestling singlet) or not trying even the smallest bit (hasn't updated the ol' wardrobe

since high school or even washed the prom puke off his jeans).
He's generally unafraid to accentuate whatever is particularly
different or conventionally ugly.

- *Common occupations:* Those that can divert suspicious, tired,
  unhappy people from the way they feel and part them from
  their money, e.g., tour guides, stockbrokers, maître d's, and
  entertainers (which can include those who wait tables, temp,
  or work at any job usually held by someone who'd rather be
  making a living in the arts). Also, those who need an outlet for
  ADD, such as salesmen and politicians.
- *What attracts you first:* The pleasure of being entertained, the
  relief of not having to think up entertaining or interesting things
  to say yourself, and the wicked joy of identifying common pet
  peeves and mortal enemies and secretly tearing them a new
  asshole.
- *Red flags:* Noticing that the same jokes get repeated with
  everyone, that he may have a malicious edge that might easily
  target you when you're not in the room, that you aren't getting
  to know much about his work or relationships, that funny
  periods are sometimes followed by angry/sad periods where he
  confesses to a great deal of self-loathing and self-doubt, or that
  the funnies don't stop even when they're less funny and more
  inappropriate.

### Seeking Humor

Unless you truly want to be left alone to stew and write your manifesto, a person with a good sense of humor is hard to resist. By entertaining you without requiring any effort in return, a funny person
draws you in, promising easy access to friendship and more fun to

come. While nothing is necessarily wrong with enjoying someone's sense of humor and finding her instantly attractive and easy to talk to, don't think finding a funny person means you're always going to have fun together. Remember the procedures you've developed to keep yourself from harm while getting to know someone, no matter how hard it is to keep a serious perspective (or a straight face).

Here are three examples:

- *One of the things I like most about my girlfriend is that she's funny and quick to laugh about and get over problems and conflicts. The trouble is, when I want to talk seriously about something, like whether we're going to stay together next year when her work assignment ends or how she feels about our future in general, she always avoids the conversation by making light of the subject, so I can't tell where she stands. My goal is to get her to be serious about her real opinions when it's important.*

- *I think my boyfriend is funny, but sometimes I'm the only person who does. I can tell that my friends get annoyed by his jokes, and my parents think he's disrespectful, but I think they all need to lighten up. My goal is to get everyone to appreciate his humor as much as I do.*

- *I'm attracted to my girlfriend because she makes me laugh a lot, so I know we share something special. However, she never seems to turn it off, so I'm not sure that I'm getting to know her. It can also be exhausting and annoying because, if we're just watching TV or driving to the movies, she doesn't need to be working so hard to entertain me and put on a show. My goal is to figure out a way to put her at ease so we can get to know each other.*

It's wonderful to find a relationship full of easy laughter, entertainment, and warm feelings of acceptance, but when anything comes too easily, especially in the beginning, it should be cause for alarm. That's because, sooner or later, good relationships require hard work to endure hard times, so you have to ignore all the mirth and laughter and consider whether this person is still going to be there when the laughter stops and still be willing to start laughing again whenever the storm passes.

You've certainly discovered a valuable quality if you have a girlfriend who's quick to get over conflicts and laugh about problems, particularly if she can maintain this high level of chill during the most stressful situations, e.g., when you're in an airport on day two of waiting for an indefinitely delayed flight to visit your ailing aunt while also recovering from a bout of norovirus. In that case, you've found a great companion, but, from what you've said, not necessarily a great partner.

While you don't need to know her opinion about the national debt or political parties, you do need to know what she wants to do with her life, whether she wants to do it with you, and what she's done with relationships in the past. Humor and affability are great, but not enough, and maybe too much if they get in the way of doing the work of making a life together.

If she can't provide answers to serious questions, rely on detective work to look for the truth. No, it won't tell you whether she loves you or wants to marry you, but it will tell you whether she's a loyal friend, has made compromises to share a life with former boyfriends, has managed debt and savings responsibly, and is generally serious about being a good person and building a solid life and career. Hopefully, even though she avoids serious talk, her other behaviors will reveal a secret serious person with a good sense of humor, rather than a person who uses humor to hide an inability to make serious decisions.

A special intimacy comes from sharing a weird, quirky sense of humor, particularly when most people, including your parents, don't get it. It's a relief to find a fellow alien who actually comes from your comedy home planet and shares your customs and sensibilities. Unfortunately, a common sensibility doesn't guarantee good character, and your family's negative response to your boyfriend's humor may not just be a matter of taste. Ask them to explain what they find offensive, then ask yourself whether his jokes could cause trouble in work situations or with mutual friends.

While you may feel particularly needed by someone who doesn't get along well with others, as well as more secure about his fidelity, you need a partner who does not repeatedly alienate people at work or make it hard for you and him to develop mutual friends. A pet skunk can be a close companion if you feel rejected and helps you feel more protective than despised, but it doesn't make it easier to make a living, build a warm social circle, or have any friends outside of those in the tomato-juice industry.

As for dating someone who's perpetually funny in an entertaining way but can't seem to turn it off, you're right to wonder whether she can be comfortable on a more intimate level. In the beginning it's fun and flattering, particularly if she's funny and trying hard to please. It's tempting to assume that you're the one who can eventually ease her insecurity and help her drop her mask and be herself.

Unfortunately, not all entertainers have a solid personality behind the mask; sometimes they can't get over the anxiety of intimacy, and sometimes there's just nothing there. They will always see life as one long improv game, and in the world of improv, the word "no" is discouraged, so any attempt to end her performance won't go over well. Don't then assume you've done something wrong if your relationship gets stuck in laugh mode and doesn't move forward. Ask yourself whether you've done your best to make her comfortable, and try to find out if others have had more success with her than you. Then you'll know whether your partner will ever feel comfortable being herself, or whether she *is* being herself, and she's just not for you.

As powerful and intimate as laughter can make you feel as you seek a special relationship, be aware of its limits; the humor that draws you together may also create a wall or present a smoke screen. Your goal, as always, is to find a partnership that can give you some good laughs, but is good for much more in the long run. So stick to the basics and hope it's a true beginning and not just an amusing anecdote you'll tell friends and future prospects.

### Quiz: Comedy Questionnaire—Is laughter distracting you from warning signs?

1.  After one night out together with her, your friends become convinced that your new girlfriend is the funniest person they're ever met and want you to get married so they can keep hanging out with her and being entertained forever. You resolve to:

    A:  End it because she grabs all the attention, but only if you can find a way to make sure she doesn't grab your friends away from you entirely.

    B:  Seconding their sentiment, you take their advice and buy a ring (despite your only having been together a month and you aren't 100 percent sure you know her last name).

    C:  Enjoy your conversations and your friends' support but try to find out more facts about her life, beyond the funny.

2. He's a funny guy and thoughtful, but you can't get him to talk about his family or past relationships in any way that doesn't involve a setup and a punch line (or does involve facts). You decide to:

A: Let him know that family and relationships, like most things, are no joke, and if he can't take his life seriously, he has no place in yours.

B: Assume that, because he's probably had some painful past relationships and definitely has superior comedy skills, he's earned the right to deflect with humor and you're happy letting it slide.

C: Redouble your efforts to do your own, not-creepy recon—find mutual acquaintances you can pump for information, do a social media search, etc.—to find out more about his relationship and work history.

3. You notice she tries to joke you out of your resentments or bad moods, and while you appreciate her trying to cheer you up, it's sometimes annoying when you simply don't want to be cheered up and feel your frustrations deserve more respect. You tell her that:

A: You've had it with her disrespect and she'd better start taking you and your pain seriously. Wait, why is she laughing?

B: You love how you've found someone who can almost always make you smile and get you to forget your troubles (even if you have no fucking idea what to do about those troubles and are willing to let her continually distract you with yucks).

C: You appreciate her interest in what's bothering you, but it's too serious to just laugh off, so what you'd like is some genuine advice.

4. When an old friend mentions your funny girlfriend's prior boyfriend in her presence, you notice she stops talking for a day, but
   when you ask her about it, she refuses to talk about him because
   thinking about him makes her so unhappy. You tell her:
   A: It's great she's finally taking her life seriously but let her know
      that if she can't share suffering with you, then she's inflicting
      it upon you twofold.
   B: You thank heaven she got over her blues in a day, respect her
      silence on the subject, and let her know you'll never bring up
      anything unhappy or unfunny ever again if she doesn't want
      you to.
   C: You tell her that you can see her feelings were complicated
      but that you can be a better friend and understand her better
      if she can tell you what happened, even if it hurts too much
      to laugh about.

5. When you finally meet his parents, your normally funny boyfriend falls silent and seems uncomfortable. The parents seem
   like nice people, but they're as uneasy with him as he is with
   them. You decide to:
   A: Grill him later on why he thinks he can't be that respectful
      and quiet all the time, especially since his parents seemed to
      raise him with a strong example of appropriate behavior.
   B: Fake a severe allergic reaction so you and your boyfriend can
      leave early and he'll feel better and get back to his usual hilar-
      ious self.
   C: Treat his parents as potential friends and ask them lots of
      neutral questions about their lives with the goal of being
      friendly, not funny.

If you answered mostly A's . . .

You have a strong humorless streak that prevents you from appreciating your partner's comedy skills and even causes you to resent them. No matter how much she shows you that she cares, her sense of humor will eventually annoy you and make you feel insecure. In the meantime, you're not finding out much about her as a person, her abilities as a potential partner, or why you're with her and not someone who shares your love of seriousness.

If you answered mostly B's . . .

You love having a personal comedy club and refuse to let anything stop the good times from rolling. You certainly won't intrude on your girlfriend's privacy or cause her any pain, but you're also unlikely to know how (or if) she will withstand tough times when tears trump laughter.

If you answered mostly C's . . .

You have positive ways of getting to know people who may hide behind humor, and you know what you're looking for, beyond a good laugh. You're happy to let him grab attention or entertain, but you're more interested in his character traits, ability to share in a partnership, and ability to reveal more about himself as time passes and his need to amuse and impress (hopefully) subsides a bit.

## Faulty Shortcuts to Funny

If you're not naturally funny, avoid these faulty methods for getting laughs:

| Don't | Why Don't |
|-------|-----------|
| Drink until you're hilarious | Because people are just laughing at you, not with you, and they're also feeling sorry for you and not sleeping with you either way. |
| Borrow jokes from your favorite late-night-show monologue | Even if you don't get caught plagiarizing, there is (A) almost no not-awkward way to insert a joke into natural conversation, and (B) no excuse for inserting humor into a conversation prefaced with "Wanna hear a joke?" unless you're under ten years old and the joke begins "Knock knock." |
| Recount, in detail, your favorite episode or the most *hilarious* episode of *Family Guy*, *Duck Dynasty*, *Murphy Brown*, etc. | Falls between "your dreams" and "work gossip about strangers" on the list of "most never-not-boring conversation topics." |
| Try your hand at physical comedy and fall down a lot | People are just as likely to find you funny as they are those who are drunk, epileptic, or in the hospital. |
| Find a random target and mock her appearance (race, weight, bowl cut) | If this works as a way to make your friends laugh, it also works as a way to know your friends are assholes (and that you're in good company). |

## Having a Good Sense of Humor

Since funny people aren't always fun to be around or work with, they rarely make good partners (as explained further on p. 127). After all, the professional funny guy who makes a living complaining about his wife in front of an audience probably goes home to lingering resentment rather than a trusting partnership. Even lay funny people have trouble with the stability marriage requires. You don't usually want a joker so much as a person whose view of life's frustrations, paradoxes, and inconsistencies is more likely to make you laugh and disarm tension rather than a person who rants, attacks, or whines about unfairness and ramps up the unpleasantness. So when it comes to a sense of humor, don't confuse possible candidates with stand-up skills for definite stand-up people.

Here are three examples:

- *My girlfriend usually laughs at my jokes, which is great, but when she doesn't, I get nervous and start to wonder what's the matter. I can't tell whether she didn't like the joke, or was offended and is now stewing over it, or is just annoyed with me and maybe our relationship. I can't ask her why she didn't like it or if something's wrong because I know that will just get on her nerves. My goal is to be able to make her laugh without having to worry about whether she does or not.*

- *As an awkward girl, I usually use humor to make social interactions easier, but if I'm trying to meet guys, being funny only gets me so far. I know most people say they want a partner with a sense of humor, but I don't know how to be seen as more than just "the funny girl" and not "a cute girl who's funny." I guess I'm overdoing it or giving out the wrong vibe, but I'm not sure how to fix it. My goal is to be the right kind of funny (i.e., the kind that doesn't neuter me or the guy I'm talking to).*

- *Like a lot of funny people, I'm not always a happy person; I get bad depressions sometimes, and when I do, the only jokes I make are dark (and maybe unsettling, and not really funny). The problem is that the girls I date are usually attracted to my sense of humor, so when I stop being funny and start being a miserable fuck, they freak out and leave. My goal is to find girls who think I'm funny but accept me when I'm not.*

Once you find you can be funny, it may be hard not to put on your funny persona when trying to meet and impress people. Hiding behind jokes seems to make you more interesting and gives you a way to prevent boredom, avoid silence, and make it easy to leave people wanting more. Such joking, however, is like using water wings or training wheels: they makes things easier at first, but you must eventually give them up if you want to acquire real skills. That's why dropping humor is the only sure way you can make authentic personal connections, even though, without it to rely on, you may drown or crash.

It's natural to become dependent upon the response you get from being funny, particularly when you're trying to impress someone you care about. Unfortunately, most funny people find it hard to connect with others and to relate to the world in general, and while being an outsider provides the skewed perspective that creates humor, it also causes a sense of isolation that makes connecting with other people extremely difficult. That's why making people laugh becomes the easiest way to relate to them, and laughter the clearest indication to someone oblivious of subtle social cues that a connection is made.

The downside is that, when laughter doesn't happen, it can compound that sense of isolation into something even more painful; comedians "die" or "bomb" if they can't get a laugh, whether it's publicly onstage or in a one-on-one situation. It's worse when silence makes you wonder whether your girlfriend is offended, annoyed, or ready to depart, so it's natural to want to reduce your anxiety by keeping her laughter flowing.

Unfortunately, the more you let fear drive your social behavior, the more it blocks a real relationship. Your uncertainty and neediness will become obvious and make your girlfriend feel responsible for your feelings, which tends to wear out the most entertaining relationship. So your goal isn't to reassure yourself that she's happy and not annoyed; it's to let her feel whatever she feels and see how her feelings mesh with yours, or not.

Sadly, you can't guarantee that she'll like you when you stop joking. What you can do is try to find interesting things to do together and live up to your own standards for being thoughtful, considerate, and a good listener. Then, even if things don't click, you'll know that you've done your best to build a relationship, have no one to blame, and will learn from the experience.

If your style of humor saps the sexiness out of your image, you may have overdeveloped your comic talents as a way of getting attention when you weren't getting it for just looking good. Anxiety and neediness are great inspirations for humor, but they tend to deflate sexual chemistry; lots of people like to laugh at the guy who jokes about jerking off or at the girl who tells fart jokes, but there's a reason that models are silent. Just as nobody can simply change their feelings, you probably can't alter what you find funny, or how humor affects your attractiveness; it's hard to order up the "right kind of funny," even when you know exactly what you want.

If you can keep anxiety and neediness in check, then you can rely less on humor and more on finding other social activities and common interests. Don't assume that humor is a hindrance and that attractiveness and frequent dating are the key to finding a partner; that would be depression talking, which, like *Mr. Show* DVDs and nearsightedness, is something every funny person is likely to have (see below). Ignore self-critical thoughts, try to find things you like to do, and look for someone who might have what it takes and also seems genuinely interested.

Using less humor may leave you feeling unnoticed and disconnected. If, however, you rate yourself more by your determination and character than by the number of laughs you get or pounds you weigh, and if you stay focused on your search for someone equally solid, you will find someone who takes you seriously and then discovers a bonus in your sense of humor.

When it comes to generating humor, depression is a double-edged sword: it can provide you with a unique perspective that cuts through sentimental platitudes and stirs the deep laughs that acknowledge pain, but it can also make you irritable and nasty while putting thoughts in your head that devalue your worth, your future, and the respect of others. It's not surprising that depression can sometimes make you attractive and at other times threaten or damage relationships. If depressed feelings make you act like a miserable human being, especially if you make no effort to manage them, you can't expect relationships to last. Even if your friends basically accept you, they shouldn't tolerate abuse. If they do, your relationships aren't healthy for you or them.

If, on the other hand, you look carefully for a friend who can tolerate your depressed moods without needing you to smile and doesn't take your unhappiness personally, and if you can also behave decently even when you feel like shit, you can find a relationship that will last. You don't have to get rid of depression to find a good relationship, but you do need the strength to control nasty behavior and to look for the right kind of person to ignore your occasional nasty thoughts.

It wouldn't hurt to do your best to figure out a way to manage your depression so that it doesn't do as much damage to your life. You may feel less funny for a while (or just feel less, period), but you have to decide whether enduring periods of painful self-hatred justifies the periods when you're the wittiest guy in the room (and too miserable to enjoy it).

Just having a good sense of humor can make you bad at finding or keeping relationships, but if you remember to value yourself for what you have to offer, not for how much you can amuse people, your humor can certainly add pleasure and maybe wisdom when you're developing and keeping close relationships with people who like you as a person, not just as a performer.

### Jerks and Jokes—Why So Many Comedians Are Miserable Assholes

Unless you live in New York, Los Angeles, or an airport hotel, you have probably had little direct contact with professional comedians. Most of us have met funny people, such as that cousin who does the meanest running commentary at family weddings or the guy at the office whose MS Paint skills make group projects bearable, but these are civilians who are good at getting laughs. There's a difference between being a funny cousin, brand manager, or orthodontist and being funny for a career. The former are funny for fun, and most of the latter are funny because their miserable lives depend on it.

By and large, professional comedy types, be they stand-up comedians, improvisers, or just writers (ahem), aren't just funny for a living, but have chosen this living because they believe it utilizes the one skill they have, a skill developed to overcome an otherwise crippling shyness, tragedy, or sense of otherness. They are funny because their ability to function depends on it. They often need laughter so as to feel whole, which is a good motivation for surviving in the competitive world of professional comedy, but a terrible way to live your life if you don't want to hate and doubt yourself 99 percent of the time.

Since most of us have also met depressed people—that other cousin who always gives the angry-drunk toasts at weddings, or the guy at work whom you often catch staring into space or crying in the bathroom—we know how unpleasant they are to be around. However, unlike your garden-variety depressives, who just hate themselves, most comedians have the confusing mind-set of "I hate myself; *why doesn't everybody love me?*" Then they hate themselves for the desperation that pushes them to get onstage all the time and work their asses off for approval and success—just as much as they hate the people who *do* love them for being stupid enough to love such a miserable asshole.

We're sure that some comedians are actually well-balanced, confident, highly functional individuals—maybe those guys who used to define their comedy by the blueness of their collar, or those YouTube comedy stars whose core audience is ages eleven to twelve, or, inexplicably, ventriloquists. But in reality, the funniest comedians can be the biggest bummers to be around. Then again, if most comedy people weren't miserable, they'd have way better stuff to do than kill themselves making all us assholes laugh.

## Humor and Marriage

When you've come to depend on a partner's humor, the absence of humor can feel like the loss of marital happiness. Your marriage may still be healthy without humor, however, just as it may be unhealthy with it. A fun parent isn't always good one, and a grumpy spouse isn't always a bad partner. So never assume that someone who is fun to be with will ensure you a jolly marriage, or define marriage by the way it makes you feel, whether that feeling is loving, lustful, or full of laughter.

Here are three examples:

- *I've always liked my husband's sense of humor, but now that we have kids, he enjoys joking with them and leaving all the negative stuff for me, which forces me to be bad cop to his eternal good cop. It's not fun for me, and I resent that the kids can't wait for him to get home but see me as a grouch or their prison warden. My goal is to get him to stop the joking around all the time and share in the tough part of parenting.*

- *My wife was happy and funny until her sister died, then she got a depression that still hasn't lifted. Now she seldom smiles and is often angry, and therapy doesn't seem to help. I miss the woman I married and don't like this humorless, pissed-off version nearly as much. My goal is to find a way back to our old relationship.*

- *I fell in love with my husband's sense of humor, though I knew he was funniest when he was drinking. Unfortunately, his drinking has increased over the years; he used to have fun on weekend nights only, but now that he's drinking more frequently, it's not making him any funnier, and it is starting to put a strain on our life together. He insists he still just drinks for a laugh, but he's on thin ice at work and the kids notice how hungover he is. My goal is to get him to take his drinking seriously.*

It's natural to want to nourish and maintain the good feelings you get from humor (or a good night's sleep or a personal victory at work or cocaine, etc.), but it's not reasonable to feel that you should be able to maintain the laughter and good feeling indefinitely, especially in a marriage. Otherwise, when something happens that makes laughter impossible—which, in any long-term relationship, is inevitable—you'll feel like a failure and your response may well make things worse.

If the humor your husband used to share with you before you had kids is now given to them instead of you, it's hard not to feel demoted and disregarded, particularly when parenting makes you feel tired and irritable and all the not-fun parenting tasks fall on your shoulders. You were hoping for a partner who would help you see the fun in parenting, not someone who would monopolize the fun and force you to rein them all in. If you've lost faith in his ability to be a responsible parent, you're also likely to put even more responsibility on yourself, which deepens your resentment.

Your partner might listen if a mutual friend or family therapist warns him that his joking with the kids undermines his responsibilities and endangers his marriage. It's just as likely, however, that any criticism will make him feel more aligned with the kids as leader of the persecuted group of scolded fun-lovers and increase the distance between the two of you. If that's the case, give him more opportunities to do solo parenting, even if you don't like the way he does it or don't feel comfortable putting him in charge. After all, you have no control over his parenting if you're separated or divorced, and you have good reason to believe he's not totally incompetent (and if you don't, you have a better reason to wonder why you married him in the first place). Withhold your criticism even if you see him make mistakes or believe the kids are harder to manage after he hands them back.

With luck and a little time, he'll have to deal with the less attractive parts of parenting and figure out his own methods for managing difficult behavior, other than laughing at your attempts to control it. Meanwhile, you'll get a chance to relax and watch him learn the hard way. You may never regain the lighthearted companionship of your preparenting days, but if you can tolerate his parenting style and still believe you're benefiting from his contributions, you may have good reason to feel you have a good marriage.

Losing your wife's laughter to severe depression can also feel like a personal loss, even when you know the reason for the depression or, at least, know the reason isn't you. Your helplessness may cause you to feel you should be able to cheer her up, or, if your efforts fail, to blame her for having issues with oversensitivity, overattachment, or insufficient time with a shrink. Depression can happen to people who have good marriages and senses of humor, and, indeed, a good sense of humor may be a risk factor (see p. 126). In addition, support from friends or a therapist is no guarantee of a cure. So don't let your wishes for the old rapport or expectations about controlling depression make you critical, because you'll just make the situation worse.

Instead, accept the pain and respect the good efforts you've both made to survive it. As long as you can control your expectations and anger, you can help her fight the negative ideas depression puts in her head, widen her knowledge of what does and doesn't help, and urge her to try any treatment that offers a reasonable hope of improvement. Maybe you can't get the laughter back, but if you can accept the person who is living with depression, you can forge a strong partnership that can tolerate life's sorrows.

A kind of humor can flourish with drug use that can be as addictive as the drugs that make it possible. If that's the humor that brought you and your husband together, then it's understandably difficult for you to confront him about alcohol use, even though you see it escalating and interfering with the responsibilities of adult life. In addition, if you're critical, he'll remind you of how much you liked his party persona before, accuse you of trying to change him, and threaten to take the good times away. So, no, there's no way you can expect to hang on to the fun drunk while getting him to stop drinking, and it won't help to criticize him for not being able to be sober and still funny.

Your first job then is to put aside your dependence on alcoholic gaiety and decide if the sober guy would be a decent partner, even if less fun. Then, whether you decide to stay or leave, you're ready to give him constructive advice. Let him know that, as much as you appreciate his fun side, you now know his way of enjoying life is destructive to his long-term partnership, job, family, and health. Sobriety may make him dull and unhappy and may even drive you away, but it's still better than the alternative. You hope he sees what you mean.

It's great to begin a marriage with humor, but if a marriage is to last and do what you need it to do, it must tolerate the times when laughter is impossible. So don't overrate laughter as a value or goal of marriage, but accept it as a welcome dividend, like the special humor that can only develop over years from sharing good times *and* hardships, together.

### Did You Know . . . Truth, or Bullshit?

*We examine widely accepted beliefs about relationships to determine whether they're true (or not so much). The phrase in question:* "What women look for most in a man is a sense of humor."

"A sense of humor" may be what women say they most look for in a man, at least when asked by lady magazines or the pollsters at *Family Feud*, but this notion is hard for many men to believe; skeptics believe that women only say this to be nice, and that, if they were being honest, they'd favor a more superficial trait. Many (fairly humorless) men argue further that what women look for most is a guy with a hot bod, a sweet ride, a fat bank account, or any other icky adjective-and-noun pairing that's unflattering to everyone, because women are just as shallow as men and no sane woman would choose a prop comic over a personal trainer (although the world's premier prop comic, Carrot Top, is now built like a personal trainer, but that's beside the point).

While prima facie the guy with a tight five-minute set would lose to a guy with tight abs, a "sense of humor" doesn't necessarily mean "comedian" or even "normal guy whom I find to be hilarious." No woman wants to be with a guy who has *no* sense of humor—who, like the angry jerks described above, is humor*less*—because besides being less than fun, humorless people are quick to anger, and men that are quick to anger tend to get violent. And if there's one thing most women don't look for, it's a guy who chooses fists over funny.

So, guys, if you're neither handsome nor hilarious, don't worry. Sure, it helps to be either or both, but the key to appealing to women is being quick to laugh, especially at yourself, and to face crises with ease rather than easily freaking out or picking a fight.

VERDICT: NOT (EXACTLY) BULLSHIT

Laughter is like conversational lube; it makes getting to know or be with someone easy and frictionless, but only for so long. When it eventually wears away, you'll need a more permanent, reliable way of finding a good partner and working on the hard issues that life presents. Enjoy humor, but don't idealize it or let it stop you from evaluating people by their other qualities and actions instead of their quips. If you don't let humor distract you from the serious process of finding a partner with a strong character and compatible goals, you will find something far more long lasting to smile about.

| What to Look For | What to Achieve/What Not to Be Fooled By |
| --- | --- |
| Mutual attraction | . . . in part, from a shared appreciation of the same jokes and an ability to laugh at things that are painful and not mainly from laughing at the things you both despise or are afraid of. |
| Mutual respect | . . . that comes from your shared ability to accept and laugh at your weaknesses while calmly accepting those of others, no matter how tough it gets, and not from your talent for getting laughs from a tough crowd. |
| Shared effort | . . . that continues even when there's no way either of you can smile, let alone laugh, rather than from trying to one-up each other's amusing banter. |
| Common interests | . . . in activities that do not necessarily require fun, laughs, amused third parties, and/or a designated driver. |
| Common goals | . . . such as figuring out how to spend time together, not when you can include friends and fun, but when you're tired, fed up, irritable, and as unamusable as you can get. |

# Five Ways to Tell If a Relationship Has Staying Power

1. *Quantify your quality connection time:* While the hours of look-ing into each other's eyes, endless deep conversations, and entire weekends spent naked may seem overwhelmingly significant, those moments don't tell you much. Instead, total up the min-utes when you don't have much to say and aren't feeling partic-ularly needy, lusty, or chatty, but like spending time with each other doing nothing much at all.

2. *Rate your ability to protect your time together:* Most people worry that their spouse will destroy their relationship with a secret affair; more frequently, however, the real threat to relationships are very public, overly responsive connections to parents, exes, bosses, etc. If you're with someone who prioritizes your relationship ahead of the needs of his chummy or needy exes, grown kids, or at least one nutty parent, then you may have a future ahead of you.

3. *Consider whether this relationship is copacetic with the major life goals of both of you:* No amount of mutual love and affection can sustain a relationship if one party is always out of town, mov-ing from city to city, or risking life and limb, and the other party just wants deep roots, constant company, and a partner with all limbs intact. Remember, love can't change character, and if someone's character moves her in a unique path that the other can't accept, you can't move forward together.

4. *Try overcoming a major challenge together:* Nothing tests the mettle of a relationship like jointly taking on a tough situation,

e.g., a trip to the emergency room, a backpacking trip through Patagonia, a fight over whether the novels of Susan Sontag are brilliant or self-indulgent, overrated crap. Watch to see what shape you're in when you get through, as well as whether your partner includes you and asks for help when he faces a major loss or setback.

5. *Live with your partner:* Move in and see if he or she will give you closet space, do the dishes, replace the empty toilet-paper roll without being asked; overcoming a specific obstacle or tragedy or argument is one thing, but getting through a series of daily struggles is a test like none other. To up the ante, get a puppy with a nervous stomach, or move into a house that needs major repairs, or go live somewhere you have no other friends or barely know the language. There's no better way than sharing space to figure out if you share enough fundamental values and complementary traits to spend the rest of your lives together.

# Chapter 6

# F*ck Good Family

There's no easy way to describe someone who has a positive relationship with her family (which hopefully doesn't consist of drunks, convicts, or people with horrifying genetic diseases). "Family stability" doesn't exactly sum it up, nor does "positive parental relationship," which is more confusing and creepy. Even though "good family" sounds like something sought by those searching for a mate with a *Downton Abbey*–style pedigree and we doubt this book will be big with the Dowager Countess set, the term will have to do.

Searching for a partner with a good family means looking for someone who has a strong relationship with a loving family who provided her with a stable upbringing, or just someone who doesn't pretend her parents are dead and whose family visits don't have to take place at supermax prisons.

Some good partners can rise above dubious beginnings, forgive their parents, and maintain contact. However, when a possible partner reveals that she was raised by wolves after her parents left her in a cave on a drunken dare or hasn't spoken to her family since being ceremonially shunned twenty years ago for reasons she doesn't want to talk about, it should make you wonder what kind of parent she'd make, or what kind of issues her upbringing has burdened her with that could affect your life together.

Some people are drawn to good family pedigrees and some to family-trauma refugees, and logic doesn't shape their choices other than to frame the after-the-act rationalization. The good family seekers say they're looking for the aforementioned stability and child-rearing advantages, which is valid but not nearly as important as a would-be partner's character. Those drawn to damaged refugees explain that they feel an additional closeness and helpfulness because their loving relationship is healing old wounds, ignoring the risk that the old wounds are not the healing kind.

Getting to know someone's family is usually a great way to get to know who she is and what it will be like to raise a family with her. Be aware, however, that family stability isn't always the best indicator of future relationship stability.

Sometimes the family relationships that are particularly enjoyable while dating cause problems later on, and some relationships that are obnoxious or difficult now also reveal a partner's strengths. Having a stable family yourself may create unrealistically high expectations for a partnership or make it harder for you to integrate new relationships with those you have. Be aware of your prejudices and reflexes and don't let them determine your choices until you've developed a good, solid method for evaluating family relationships and their likely impact on your life together. Learn to assess weaknesses and risks that can arise from family stability (yours or a prospective partner's), predict their possible impact on a long-term relationship, and determine whether you can protect yourself from that impact if need be.

In managing family relationships, be they with your own difficult clan or with a partner's, establishing strong boundaries is the best way to prevent either of you from reacting to parents more than you react to each other or your shared and individual priorities. More important than whether you like your partner's parents or get along with them well is how well the two of you manage your differences in responding to parental guidance, pressure, guilt, or just invitations to family get-togethers. You may love your partner to pieces, but that love will be endangered if he seems to listen to his parents' advice more than yours or enjoys spending time with them more than he does with you.

When you meet a prospective partner's parents, you're not just trying to please them (though it doesn't hurt if you do); you're evaluating what they will be like as in-laws for support, intrusiveness, neediness, and influence. Don't neglect any opportunity to gather information or elicit the opinions of others who have married into the family and dealt with its leaders and their leadership style.

If you suspect cultural differences—and the risk goes up with prospective partners who come from families, regions, and cultures that you know nothing about—your evaluation must include an element of anthropology as you try to figure out the norms and rituals of regular get-togethers, religious customs, and the role of those who marry in. Never assume that love will sweep those differences away.

Someone's having a good family is not necessarily a good enough reason to commit to the person, though liking and admiring a partner's family is a good place to begin. Develop careful methods for assessing a prospective family's values, the boundaries of your possible partner's relationships with it, and the way it may influence your life together before deciding whether you have found a good fit.

Good families can drive you crazy and apart, and bad families can have almost no impact on your future lives together. Your job is to put the facts together until you understand what influence your partner's family, good, bad, or in between, will have on the stability of the life (and possible family) you build together.

## The Good Things You Want Someone from a Good Family to Deliver

- A friendly, accepting welcome from the clan that gives you everything you always wanted but have never received from your own family, or even from a visit to an Olive Garden.
- A confirmation that your prospective partner is every bit as nice, calm, and loving as she seems to be, thus guaranteeing acceptable offspring.
- A word from her parents or sibs supporting, praising, and generally marveling at how reasonable you are when she goes off the rails.
- A promise of strong financial and child-care support and an ever-ready beach house whenever you need it.
- A clean bill of family health for mental illness, substance abuse, and cystic acne.

## Profile of the Family Man or Woman

Here is a list of traits associated with someone with a solid family tree:

- *Physical attributes:* Beyond his beloved mama's nose or his admired papa's chin, his general look should reflect his place in his loving family, depending on whether he fits in with the

clan. So your good family kid either cuts a confident look, as if
he takes socializing for granted, is comfortable with adults and
strangers, and knows his place in the world, or he dresses like
an oddball, wishing he knew why he didn't belong but unable
to find a way to blame his perfectly nice family for his angst and
all-black wardrobe.

- *Common occupations:* A good family prepares you for a job
  persuading the relatively rich and comfortable that they should
  trust you because you're one of them; just having the right last
  name can open up opportunities and memberships in clubs
  and secret societies unavailable to most. If your family name is
  dirt, you can still convince fellow less fortunate outsiders that
  they should trust you because you feel their pain and know
  the importance of sticking together. Those with strong family
  support, financial or otherwise, become money managers,
  fund-raisers, golf-club and condo-board chairmen, and terrible
  US presidents.
- *What attracts you first:* Perhaps it's the sweet way he respects
  his mother or the way her family seems to immediately accept
  you as their long-lost son when she takes you to one of their
  weekly dinners. You get the impression that the parents raised
  their child right, sending a moral, baggage-free adult into the
  world who would likely also be good at raising kids right.
- *Red flags:* Noticing that your prospective partner's interests and
  opinions rarely stray from the family party line or background
  or culture and don't reflect an individual point of view based on
  his own experience. He may generally overly respect authority
  and require a bit of spine reinforcement, especially to respect
  your needs over his parents'. Most troubling, she pushes you
  to fit in with her family rather than enjoying the ways that you
  don't.

## Seeking Good Family

Of all the traits people inherit from their parents, the ability to be good parents or create a home as stable as the one they grew up in is not one that always gets passed down to the next generation. That's why, when you seek someone from a strong family, you shouldn't expect his or her family goodness to envelop you and the family you wish to start. Instead, check out how well you and your prospective partner agree on the way you experience your relationships with significant family members and believe they should be treated. Undoubtedly, seeing people in the context of their families is a great way to get to know them, but even when you think the families are wonderful, what you often discover are significant differences in the ways you respond that can't simply be negotiated out of existence, into harmony, or into line with the parenting DNA you'd come to expect.

Here are three examples:

- *I love my boyfriend's mother—everybody does, she's just that kind of person—but my love for her drives my boyfriend crazy because she wasn't the greatest mother to him and his feelings are much less positive or clear-cut. That everybody, not just me, thinks she's the best makes him both angry and insecure. My goal is to get along with my boyfriend's family without getting my boyfriend annoyed.*

- *My girlfriend loves her parents, but her father totally hates me, and while my girlfriend says he's often hard on her boyfriends, she won't admit that he hates every guy she's ever been with just on principle. I don't want to talk shit about him because he means everything to her, but I don't see how we can stay together if someone she loves so much thinks I'm such an asshole. My goal is to figure out how to get her beloved father off my back.*

- *I was excited to meet my girlfriend's family because she'd talk all the time about them and how fun and nice they are, but when I met them, I was horrified. Her parents and siblings yell at each other and cut each other down constantly, and everything they say to one another is nasty. I don't know how she can consider that house of horrors to be loving, but she does, and it makes me question her judgment and what she can offer a family of her own. My goal is to make sense of what my girlfriend's misperception of her Manson family means.*

While a family may run as a positive, amiable unit, it's still made up of individuals who have distinct tastes and points of view and unique sets of chemistry within the group. Even the most stable family can be a fragile ecosystem, so as natural as it is to assume that people who have stable, positive relationships with their families are more likely to have such a relationship with you, those relationships may be more steady than the sum of complicated, possibly shakier parts.

So, when you finally do get to know your partner's individual family members, your response to certain members may be much more positive or negative than your prospective partner's, and certain family members' response to you may be far from what you would wish. You'll realize that the family that seemed so loving and cohesive may be split over how certain members feel about one another and about outsiders such as you.

As little control as we have over other people, we have even less over groups of people, especially those who are related, and the closer the family, the stronger the influence these differences in personal chemistry will have over your future life together.

If you see your boyfriend's mother more positively than he does, for example, you probably can't talk him into giving up his resentment and criticism, and trying may well make him feel that you don't understand him or can't accept him for who he is. So don't try to become a helpful peacemaker before thinking carefully about how your good intentions may affect the relationship that matters most—not his with his mama, but yours with him.

First, examine what he does with his negative feelings about his mother, noting carefully whether they make him mean, vengeful, sulky, or just politely distant. Watch whether he needs you to echo his point of view or is comfortable with your not sharing his feelings. You'll have reason to be more optimistic about your relationship with him if he can behave well in spite of his negativity and doesn't demand support or understanding.

If, however, their relationship is an open wound, his anger is overt, and his need for support makes him overbearing, you must find out whether he can control himself. One of your children is likely to resemble his mother, and you don't want to spend your energy running protective interference between them.

Let him know you accept that he doesn't like his mother and assume he has good reasons, but you believe it's important to maintain a civil relationship through polite, brief, and infrequent interactions. So you think he should keep his cool and not expect you to share negative feelings that are just not part of your experience with his mother. Hopefully, you'll discover that he can accept reasonable boundaries, knowing that you're not taking his mother's side but that you're also unwilling to encourage angry behavior. If not, you now know that he has a character weakness that may impact you in other ways, even if you and he live far away from his parents.

If your girlfriend's loving dad hates you, you have a right to be worried and disappointed. Don't waste time trying to win him over, particularly if it appears that your efforts are futile and just make him meaner. Also don't try to persuade your girlfriend that her father is a bad guy, because fighting for her primary loyalty will cause conflict and increase his influence over your relationship.

Instead, don't make her relationship with her father your problem unless she does. You may share her disappointment that the two of you don't hit it off, but never show that disappointment when he's around. Behave well and make it clear that when necessary you can smile your way appropriately through short family get-togethers, but let her know that you don't think longer stays are in the cards, given the unfortunate chemistry.

You hope, however disappointed she is that he doesn't like you, that she doesn't respond with blame or expect you to spend more time with him than necessary. You want her to know that you won't be hurt if she spends somewhat more time with him than you do, but you also want her to regard *you* as her chief adviser and partner in your life ahead, not as a consort who stands by while she asks her father what he thinks.

If she meets those expectations, you can justifiably hope that she won't let her father's animosity interfere with the boundaries of her relationship with you. Otherwise, the problem isn't her father, it's her inability to define her own priorities and opinions, and you can expect your partnership to be troubled.

It's creepy to discover that the family your girlfriend loves and admires is, in your opinion, a bunch of not-adorable, overbearing jerks. You and she have a basic disagreement that may also reflect a difference in the way the two of you judge people that may not be possible to resolve.

What's most important, however, is not winning your girlfriend to your point of view but seeing if her admiration and love reflect a problem in her values or boundaries in all her relationships. You need to know whether her love for her jerky family means she's also drawn to jerky friends who tend to exert too much influence over her life. If so, you then need to know whether she expects you to share her taste in friends. You hope to find that her friends, including you, are not at all like her family, and that, aside from her family, she is able to identify jerky behavior and protect herself when appropriate. If so, you may want to check out her family again and ask for a second opinion from a friend, to make sure you aren't overreacting.

You also need to know that she doesn't require you to share her love for her family and can accept that, if she chooses you, you and the kids won't be spending more than the minimum amount of time required for good family diplomacy. Let her know where you stand, without implying that her family is at fault or that you feel anything other than regret that things can't be different, and see if she's amenable to your terms. Even if you can't share her feelings for her family, you can determine whether her values are better anchored than her family's and whether she can accept your thoughts for keeping your relationship with them respectful, even if it falls short of her ideal.

Sometimes a prospective partner's close family is as wonderful and simpatico as described and you all get along like gangbusters despite every mother-in-law joke, previous personal experience, and Nate Silver–style probability that would indicate otherwise. More often, though, you all get along less like gangbusters and more like rival gangs, and complications ensue.

Whether your partner has a stable family or a sucky one, dealing with them is like being a politician; success depends on pleasing a large group with differing, conflicting opinions by being as pleasant and bland as possible during rare personal appearances. You can't judge your partner by the sanity of her electorate, but watching how your partner manages them can give you valuable information about her strengths. More important, you'll be able to gauge your ability as a team to manage and tolerate differences in the way you respond to people and the stability of the ecosystem of your relationship in the long run.

### Quiz: Family Questionnaire—Are You a Fair Family Judge* When It Comes to Prospective Partners?

1. Your boyfriend's mother makes you feel genuinely welcome the first Thanksgiving you spend together, but you can't help noticing that she seems much more comfortable with your boyfriend than with his younger brother, who sits at the other end of the table, says little, and is only addressed when someone remembers something critical to say to him. You decide to:

    A: Return her obvious affection for you and your boyfriend in a bond-building exercise because she's so sweet to you and your beloved that you can ignore the weirdness of the little-brother stuff.

    B: Get so creeped out by the situation that you feign stuffing-induced diarrhea and spend the rest of the meal hiding in the bathroom, texting your boyfriend to sneak you a slice of pie.

    C: At a later time and safer distance, ask your boyfriend if there's a reason everybody's so hard on his brother or whether this is part of a bigger problem.

2. When you first meet your girlfriend's family at a birthday party they throw for her, you notice her brothers like to tease her in a

---

*While Judge Judy was a family judge, try to emulate her wisdom only, not her exact professional path.

way that doesn't seem friendly and that she doesn't much seem to enjoy. You would:

A:  To strengthen your relationship with the family, give them the benefit of the doubt and try to convince the birthday girl that they're just a couple of mooks who mean well.

B:  Tell the boys they're less funny than they think, and if they don't like your speaking up, you'll be glad to teach them respect outside and make this her happiest birthday ever.

C:  Watch how she and her parents manage her brothers' gibes, do what you can to distract them or remove her from their presence, and ask her later if they're always this charming and how she feels about it.

3.  When you first have dinner with your boyfriend and his mother, you're unsettled by the way she drinks too much and then bad-mouths his father, from whom she's divorced. You notice your boyfriend is so uncomfortable that he sits there about as silently as you do and drops out of the conversation. Your approach is to:

A:  Give his mother some attention, support, and a bottomless glass of chardonnay in an effort to get closer to her and help her get all the feelings out so that she can find some sort of peace and catharsis.

B:  Storm out, mortified by his mother's behavior, then write a positive Yelp review of the restaurant to both apologize for your boyfriend's mother and out her to the world as a bitter lush.

C:  Find out later whether this woman "wines and whines" regularly (and maybe if drowning sorrows is a wider family tradition).

4. On a visit to your boyfriend's parents in another city, you're surprised to be assigned separate bedrooms in his family's home although you're both in your late twenties. You would:

   A: Tell his parents how much you appreciate their kindness, hospitality, and efforts to protect your womanly honor.

   B: Explain to his parents that it's your body, your choice, and then find yourself a hotel room nearby (or a plane ticket back home, because this clearly isn't going to work).

   C: Look around the house for any curious or oversize or bounty of religious paraphernalia, then ask your boyfriend what the deal is with the sleeping arrangements.

5. You don't meet your girlfriend's older sister until your second visit with their lovely parents, so you're surprised when said sister is friendly to you but openly insults her father, whom you find to be extremely nice. Her father says little in response, and everyone appears embarrassed. You react by:

   A: Speaking separately to the sister's father and her, telling them both you totally get how the other one is such a jerk and that you're absolutely on each one's side, thereby hedging your bonding bets and getting in with everyone.

   B: Telling the sister she's being a monster and if this is how this family rolls, then they deserve one another but you deserve better (drop mic, leave).

   C: Changing the subject and waiting until later to get the scoop on what's up with the sister, why she has a beef with her father, and how the family deals with it (or, seemingly, doesn't).

If you answered mostly A's . . .

   You're a born beacon of love who is wonderful at charming

prospective in-laws and determined to get close to your beloved's relatives. Unfortunately, your job is not to win their affection or take responsibility for their happiness but to find out whether they're bearable in-laws, what possible traits they may have saddled your partner with, and if they can leave you and your prospective partner out of their bullshit. Stick with unconditional affection and you find yourself sucked in, stuck, and, sooner or later, targeted yourself.

If you answered mostly B's . . .

You can't stop yourself from seeing the worst in every ugly family situation, and, by extension, every partner, without first stopping to think about whether you're overreacting or what impact these situations or dynamics would have on your relationship with your partner. You may be trying to avoid problems, but you're more likely to cause them. Unless you can learn to be more patient, tolerant, and better at understanding and evaluating your prospective partner, your reactiveness to awkward family situations will keep you from being in any solid relationships, period.

If you answered mostly C's . . .

You're doing a good job of presenting yourself to your partner's family as a pleasant, unemotional nonlunatic while carefully observing the customs and trigger points of the local natives. You're learning important things about the strengths, weaknesses, and general marriageability of your current candidate.

## Family Feud: How to Judge a Prospective Partner by How He Handles Family Crises

Whether your partner's family is fancy or the first family of the trailer park, the important thing isn't what they're like or how much money they have, but what your partner's like when they start to act up. Here are some common family-related social catastrophes, for families both bad and good, and the best- and worst-case scenarios for how a partner would handle the drama.

| Situation | Good Family v. Bad Family Example | A Good Partner Would | A Bad Partner Would |
|---|---|---|---|
| Within hours of meeting them, you find yourself in the front row of a massive family argument. | A passive-aggressive snipefest filled with sighs and awkward silences v. a screaming brawl where someone ends up shirtless and the cops are called. | Keep his cool, propose something constructive, and, if diplomacy backfires, find a polite way to remove both of you from the area of impact. | Join in the fray, bring some other family member to tears, and eventually storm out, leaving you there to console his victims. |
| The parents make you an offer you must refuse, but you don't know how to without seeming rude. | They invite you on the family trip to St. Barts that you can't possibly afford v. they insist you try Grandma's squirrel-meat stew and you're suddenly vegetarian. | Invent an excuse on your behalf, create a distraction, or change the subject away from the too-pricey trip or rodent soup. | Say nothing, forcing you to stumble through an excuse like "I'm really honored, but I can't because of a (previous obligation or rare allergy or imaginary religion)." |

| Situation | Good Family v. Bad Family Example | A Good Partner Would | A Bad Partner Would |
|---|---|---|---|
| When you first meet, the mother immediately starts in on her hopes for your (shared, married, fertile) future with her son. | Many, many hints about how lovely a summer wedding would be in the Vineyard v. she instantly offers to give you her wedding dress (which was only slightly damaged when those fireworks burned down their old double-wide). | Deflect the comment with humor before changing the subject, or, if the nudging persists, declare his intention to keep discussions about your relationship from being dinner-table conversation. | Stay silent, leaving you to respond politely without committing yourself, and later, when you're alone with your partner, you can ask why he hung you out to dry and let his mother plan your possible future on your shared behalf. |
| One parent makes a statement or joke or angry speech that any sane person would find offensive. | Any mention of "those people" v. the father inadvertently plagiarizes that one old Chris Rock bit that he really, really shouldn't. | Without evident embarrassment either pivot to a semirelated, not-offensive topic ("Speaking of 'those people,' Steph Curry is killing it!") or simply refuse to respond, declaring a lack of interest or opinion before changing the subject. | Confront his parents on their prejudice and vulgarity, somehow bring you into his new, two-person equality movement, and insist you'll both storm out in disgust if no apology is forthcoming. |

| Situation | Good Family v. Bad Family Example | A Good Partner Would | A Bad Partner Would |
|---|---|---|---|
| You inadvertently say something offensive. | The mother thinks it will always be too soon for Nancy Reagan jokes, as she was a true hero v. "Three generations of our family have worked at Taco Bell, or, as you just called it, 'the bowel bomb.'" | Rescue you by redefining what you meant or taking the insult or blame for the misunderstanding on himself (e.g., "Ease up, Ron Jon, she didn't know, and Grandpappy called it the Taco Smell his whole career"). | Throw you under the bus, blaming your poor sense of humor or mental health or manners, or leave you to attempt diplomacy, even though you have no one to blame for the crisis but yourself, which makes you angrier at your partner for not having your back. |

## Having Good Family

All children have a natural desire to fit in, respect, and avoid conflict with their families, and the lucky few are rewarded with a loving, reciprocal relationship. The very lucky have a relationship that provides moral guidance and lifelong support, love, and friendship (and, possibly, a writing partnership and a book deal). As an adult, however, you can't let your basic need for your parents—their company, approval, help, or contact—get in the way of your relationship with a partner. That's why having a partner meet your parents isn't just about their approving your choice or your partner's ability to fit in; it's about both sides learning to still respect each other and be civil if approval isn't in the cards. Hopefully, your family can trust that you learned enough from them to choose the right person to build a life with, but either they accept your partner or you accept your duty to protect your new partnership from their negative feelings, no parental approval required.

Here are three examples:

- *I have a big, warm family that scares the shit out of every guy I bring home. They don't mean to be so intimidating, but there are a lot of them and they're loud, verbal, curious, and protective, so they wind up overwhelming anyone they think I'm dating. My goal is to figure out a way to date and still be close to my family without their interfering.*

- *I love my parents, and we're close, but they've made it clear that they won't approve of any man I date unless he's Korean, like us. I want to respect them, but I also don't feel it's important to keep those traditions alive and don't want to date only one kind of person. My goal is to get them to love whomever I love, just as they love me.*

- *I'm proud of my family and like to introduce them to my girlfriends, but they're friendly and wind up getting close. Then, if I decide a girlfriend and I aren't right for each other, I have to contend with my breaking up her relationship with my parents as well. They don't put pressure on me, but I hate to hurt them, and I don't want to shut them out of my dating life. My goal is to make dating decisions be less complicated.*

Getting feedback from your family about prospective partners, especially if your family is close, can feel like a smart move; after all, if we're supposed to get second opinions on medical diagnoses or possible used-car purchases, we should definitely get them on potential life partners. But just as you wouldn't go to a barista to get a second opinion on your possible tumor, it's sometimes just as unwise to go to your parents for their thoughts on whether that certain someone you like is right for you.

That's why, if your family's response to prospective partners interferes with your selecting, you must decide for yourself whether your family is a good judge of who's right or wrong for you, and what you're going to do about it.

You can't change your parents, and changing their opinions, at least through arguing, is probably just as difficult. You can, however, examine their warnings, heed them when they're right, and otherwise prevent their influence and incompetent expertise from interfering with your ability to make the best possible choice.

For instance, if your family is so loud and intrusive that it overwhelms prospective partners, it's probably impossible to get them to tone down their style, and you should never oblige yourself to protect your family and spouse from mutual complaints of pain, dislike, and vulnerability. So ask yourself how important it is for you to stay closely family-involved, or at least for you to force your partner to be as involved as you are.

It's possible, for instance, that you and your family are bound together by a business or other necessity. Or you may just love their company, don't intend to leave town, and can't imagine not getting together regularly. In that case, you need a partner who can at least tolerate your family and, preferably, appreciate what you like about them, even if he doesn't want to spend as much time with them as you do.

So make it clear to prospective partners that they don't have to love your family, but since you have no intention of divorcing or leaving them in the near future, putting up with some family contact is part of the deal. Your job isn't to make them happy with one another, but to make it clear that they will have to get along, and that you don't want to hear any complaints.

If your family requires you to choose a partner with their cultural, ethnic, or religious roots, don't let rebelliousness control your decision; the last thing you want is to choose a partner in response to your parents' reaction to what he represents rather than according to your own tastes and standards. Instead, do as you've done and assess your feelings about the importance of partnership with someone who shares your roots, both in terms of how much easier family relationships will be and whether a common background and set of values will make it easier for you to understand each other and raise your children in your old tradition (if that's important to you, not just to your parents).

Then assess the likelihood of finding a partner who meets all your basic criteria for being a nice, strong person you like and get along well with, and your likelihood of finding someone with all those qualities who also shares your roots. If you value those roots and enjoy close family ties, choosing someone who meets both requirements will always make your life easier. What often happens, however, is that you can't find the person you're looking for within your own community, and after a long dating drought and several breakups, you find a solid person from another background. If that's the case, trust your experience and know that, despite your parents' possible protestations, you've made a meaningful compromise.

If you do find someone with a different background and do decide to compromise, accept the risks of parental nonacceptance and complicated child-rearing decisions. Let your parents know that you care about their values, thoughts, and recommendations, but that you believe your decision is right and hope they will adjust in time.

Having parents who get too close to your dates and then suffer when you break up with them is unfortunate and awkward, but not a problem you should take responsibility for. After all, your parents know that your priority isn't to find them a new friend, but to find someone you can eventually work with to make a new family. Their long-term interest is that you forge a marriage that survives and prospers and provides security for their grandchildren, not that you expand their social network. Don't try to change your parents or protect them, other than to suggest that they get a dog or become more involved with their local peer group. Instead, even if they feel sad or regretful, stay focused on finding someone who is a good match for you and who can be a good partner and parent. After all, these are the selection criteria that matter most and that will work best, in the long run, for everyone.

If a prospect doesn't work out, worry less about how much your parents will miss her and more about what might have gone wrong. That way you can learn from the experience how to make a better choice next time and whether you should wait longer to bring prospects around your family. They might grumble about never getting to meet your girlfriends, but you're just sparing them from getting overattached to candidates who may not work out for you.

Having a good family can teach you a great deal about how a good partnership works, but even parents who've done right by you can be wrong about who would make a worthy partner for you. That's why it may be a mistake to try to mesh a prospective partner with the family you wish him or her to be a happy part of.

If you can keep family-related anger, disappointment, or guilt from controlling your partnership negotiations and decisions, you can make the best compromise possible between finding a good partner and finding a way to stay close to your family while everyone keeps their opinions to themselves.

## Named for Nearest and Dearest: What Certain Names Can Teach You about That Person's Family History

| Name | Examples/ Variations | Inherited Pros as a Partner | Inherited Cons as a Partner |
| --- | --- | --- | --- |
| Old Waspy name | Cape, Rutherford, Tristan, or any name that could also work for a butler or that you could picture on a college library or dorm. | Possibly a lot of money, property, and entrée into secret societies that control world economies and racing yachts. | Possibly no money (anymore), strange diseases from inbreeding, strange prejudices from generations of snobbery, so many pairs of madras golf pants. |
| So-and-so Junior (or III, IV, etc.) | Aside from the obvious, also "Tripp" (which is just a WASP term for "III," so see above). | This depends on so-and-so senior. | If only a few decades separate Joe Shmoe Senior from Joe the III, then the Shmoes may have a long history of schmimpulse control. |
| Amber | Any name where *i*'s and *y*'s and *k*'s and *c*'s are interchangeable (e.g., Tami, Krystal, Jayde, etc.) and some letters are duplicated for no obvious reason, other than a possible typo (e.g., Ambyrr, Aubree, etc.). Really, anything in the stripper family. | Has been gifted by her mother (possibly also named Amber) with a name that lets you know immediately that there's a 99 percent chance she has a mood disorder and will ruin your car or credit or life. | Can get pregnant from eye contact, will limit your diet to the lunch buffet at the strip club where she works, will teach you a lot about borderline personality disorder and bond court, and all it will cost is your sanity and well-being. |

## A Good Family and Marriage

Just as time, kids, and a single shared toilet can change your view of your spouse and marriage in general, they can also change your opinion of your in-laws; when the honeymoon period ends, it can end not just for you and your wife, but for all those who ride with her, as well. You will probably discover the truth about everyone's strengths and weaknesses, including your own. The challenge is to prevent disappointment or anger about the unfairness of painful compromises from drawing you into unwinnable conflicts. Instead, accept what experience has taught you and use your wisdom to judge the value of those compromises, both within your marriage and within the family you married into.

Here are three examples:

- *I thought my husband would be a great father because his parents are solid, but it hasn't turned out that way. He works too hard, and then when he's home, he buries himself in reading and gaming and barely says two words to me or the kids. I wonder if I should get his parents to speak to him. My goal is to get him to be a better father and husband.*

- *I liked my husband's mother at first sight, but after we got married and had kids, I found she tends to take over for me as a parent whenever she's around. She loves my kids, which is great, but she tends to smother them and not follow my rules. If I get angry about it, my husband gets upset and says I'm ungrateful for her help. My goal is to not let my mother-in-law take over my job.*

- *My mother-in-law sounded fine from my wife's description, but I barely met her before we married. After our kids arrived, she*

*moved closer, and I found out she's a sad pothead who likes to*
*hang out at our house, eat our food, and tell her daughter all her*
*troubles, conspiracy theories against her, and generally babble*
*until she's ready to pass out or smoke more weed. I don't want to*
*criticize her or cause conflict with my wife, but I don't like her or*
*see her as a positive influence on our young kids. My goal is to*
*keep her from taking over our family.*

For most people, one of the great gifts and curses of being around
family is that you're not required to be polite. For dysfunctional
families, this results in free-flowing insults and anger (and occasional injuries), but for close families, this means you have a loving group you can joke with, relax around, and fart in front of with
ease. And if being overly frank and open does lead to conflict, your
closeness can make those conflicts easier to resolve; disagreements
with mere acquaintances such as roommates tend to simmer with
dirty looks and passive-aggressive notes by the dirty dishes before
there's even a confrontation, but close family can quickly call one
another on their bullshit, knowing what the limits of each are and
that, no matter how much yelling, they're still family and will eventually get over it.

The problem with in-laws is that they exist in a social gray area:
they're family, so you do share a bond, but they're not *your* family,
so you can't cut loose, cut the bullshit, or "cut one" around them the
way you can with your blood-related clan. You don't know their history the same way, which means you might misjudge the influence
they'll have on your spouse and not end up with the family you bar-
gained for (but may now be eternally bound to through your kids).

Ultimately, your shared objectives, combined with the family bonds you don't share, make you less like family and more like

coworkers. That's why your best approach to conflict resolution is to embrace the boss role, managing the relationships between your little family and the greater one with a detached professionalism that is more formal than spontaneous family fun.

If, for example, your husband's family is great and you see he's inherited their hard-worker gene, you'll be caught off guard if, unlike the rest of his tribe, he's unable to multitask with other priorities and, after a hard day's work, has little to contribute at home to you or the kids.

Instead of driving him farther into his shell by voicing your disappointment, go into business-manager mode and frame those concerns positively. After expressing admiration for his hard work at the office, ask him what he expects from himself as a husband and father, based on what he admires about his own father and fathers in general, and whether he is meeting those expectations. The more businesslike the conversation, the less defensive he's likely to become.

Don't assume that anyone else can conduct this discussion better than you can; if you push him to talk to a shrink or his parents, he may minimize the extent of his withdrawal at home, and they may have a hard time figuring out whether he's as absent as you say or whether you're feeling needy and disappointed. It helps if you can present the facts confidently, minus the resentment.

Don't feel obliged to lie about your being angry and disappointed, but don't let it become a topic for discussion. Your point isn't that you're angry and want to feel better; it's that you're concerned about the impact of his interpersonal behavior on the family and wish that he would review it as objectively as possible so he can decide whether he believes it's a problem. If he doesn't see it as a problem, don't expect him to change in order to make you happy.

With that agenda in mind, keep track of the nature and duration of his daily family-related activities and then offer to review his patterns with him and a shrink, his parents, or anyone else you both respect. What you want is not a discussion about feelings, but about whether his behavior is off the end of the bell curve and is likely to damage relationships he values. As long as you can control your feelings and observe and present facts, you may help your husband develop motivation for changing his behavior. Otherwise, at least you know you've done your best and can figure out how to move forward, with or without him.

Mothers-in-law are always a mixed bag, and in this second example the mix of the bag is not as bad as it could be. The upside is her willingness to provide child care when you've got other things to do that are necessary and important, but the downside is that she's overstepping her in-law boundaries by rejecting your parenting rules. If you let your frustration show, your anger triggers your husband into defending his mother; after all, he benefits from her child care, you're the source of anger, not she, and he's not as sensitive as you are to her intrusiveness since she's doing just fine by the boundaries he grew up with. The danger is that your frustration will trigger his defensiveness in a vicious cycle.

Instead of airing your feelings, put the ol' boss hat on and develop a set of rules that will create a new set of boundaries and give you as much control as you need, assuming that you also believe your mother-in-law should continue to contribute. Define rules of behavior that are necessary and set hours when you don't wish to be disturbed. Then present them to your husband and then your mother-in-law as a positive solution that will reduce friction. They're not meant as an expression of blame or rejection, but as an improvement that clarifies basic rules and areas of responsibility.

Discovering that your unexpectedly weak, dependent pothead mother-in-law has attached herself to your new family is certainly a challenge, but it may have been unavoidable; even if your wife was well aware of her mother's weaknesses, she may have felt too responsible for supporting and protecting her to say no or set a firm boundary. Now that your mother-in-law has come to hang out, your objections, if stated critically or with anger, are likely to make your wife more protective and cause conflict in your marriage, which will make you resent your mother-in-law all the more. So beware the dangerous, vicious cycle of expressing honest mother-in-law resentment, especially if your wife cannot easily fix the underlying problem.

Instead, give thought to your beliefs about good child care, good parenting, and the time you and your wife need to nurture a good marriage. Instead of venting fears about your mother-in-law's bad influence, put forward Grandma visitation rules that will protect the kids from inappropriate behavior. Urge your wife to define the amount of one-to-one time her mom and the kids need with one another. Then ask her whether limiting her mother's time with the family will do any real harm, other than cause painful feelings that Grandma should be managing by becoming sober and independent. Don't express resentment about your wife's unavailability because her stoned mother sucks up her time.

Like any good manager, express confidence in your vision of a better set of rules while urging your wife to sign on. Yes, you have negative feelings about her mother, but they don't distract you from your more important goal, which is for her mother to have a positive experience as a grandmother, to contribute in appropriate ways, and to feel supported. But first she needs rules to prevent her from undermining what you and your wife believe is good for the kids and your own relationship.

When you encounter unexpected problems with your family, in-laws, or your partner's character, don't let disappointment, anger, and criticism control your choices. Even strong partners and families have weaknesses that you couldn't possibly have perceived or anticipated when you were getting to know them. Evaluate problems, not by how much they irritate or upset you, but by how much they interfere with what you believe are the necessities for a good family life. Then devise good management solutions and present them positively.

Many in-law-related problems are disappointing, irritating, and unfair but can nevertheless be well managed, even if they can't be worked through as quickly (and frankly, and loudly) as they could be within your immediate family. Making a new family is hard work, so employ techniques you've acquired in the workplace to effectively manage your new relatives as you work toward the shared goal of just getting along.

### Did You Know . . . Truth, or Bullshit?

*We examine widely accepted beliefs about relationships to determine whether they're true (or not so much). The phrase in question:*
"We all end up marrying our parents."

Whether you were close to your parents or currently have a restraining order against them, lots of people are convinced that your parents program you to look for partners who remind you of them. The idea is, if your mother was overbearing, you end up marrying a ballbreaker, or if your father was a drunken asshole, you find yourself looking for love at last call. If your mother was strong and thoughtful or your father was a kind pragmatist, then you've

got a good mold to work from, but either way, the notion is that we have less free will than we think in picking our partners for life.

While people do search out the familiar, even if what they're familiar with is painful and destructive, ways exist to break old patterns and reset your search. They require a lot more discipline, patience, and willingness to withstand periods of loneliness, but if you're determined enough to stop dating cold fish like your mom or mopey jerks like your dad, then you can break the cycle and create a marriage that's unlike the one you grew up around.

No matter how you feel about your parents, you don't have to fall into the trap they set for the next generation; with some hard work and careful screening, you can break the family curse that determines what a spouse should be.

VERDICT: BULLSHIT

A good family is an attractive asset when you evaluate someone for a long-term relationship, but it's not a guarantee that your partner will have all his or her family's strengths or that those strengths won't also present problems when you all have to work together. Don't let your wish to please a family or your delight in their qualities or loving acceptance interfere with learning more about your partner's individual character and ability to set and respect boundaries in a situation that usually reveals them. Then use that information to make a good decision about whether to partner up or how to make the most of the partnership you have and the family that comes with it.

| What to Look For | What to Achieve/What Not to Be Fooled By |
| --- | --- |
| Mutual attraction | . . . from seeing each other as cofounders of a new family, with its own dynamic, set of rules, and no more than limited responsibilities to the families you came from because their appealing nature is nice but not all that important. |
| Mutual respect | . . . that comes from observing how each of you manages the tough and ugly parts of family life, rather than from how well you project a loving, attractive, impressive image to the outside world. |
| Shared effort | . . . that accepts the other person's right to his own feelings for his own family and vice versa, as long as those feelings don't cause bad behavior or familywide warfare. |
| Common interests | . . . in building a family that lives up to your standards, no matter what your parents expect or what you were raised to expect by parents who were substandard by any measure. |
| Common goals | . . . such as enjoying family when possible, given your joint priorities and common values, rather than visiting as a holy obligation to avoid a near-deadly dose of blame from parents, regardless of your other needs or the amount of pain it may cause your spouse. |

# Should My Partner and I Break Up?

Figuring out whether you should end things with your not-legally-bound partner* is never a happy process, but it is a process nonetheless, even if it feels like a mystical, chaotic form of ancient torture. You first need to figure out the value of your relationship by looking at actions, not trying to read minds, and, if it's not up to snuff, whether the bad behavior can be managed and the partnership improved. If it can't be, then you have to decide whether you have a strong reason to stay in the relationship even if it'll never be that great. If it's any consolation, as processes go, figuring out whether to end things is easy; the hard part is actually separating and goes far beyond where any flowchart could lead.

---

*This chart isn't intended for married couples because there are so many added complications to figuring out divorce, and we don't have the budget for a flowchart the size of a king-sized duvet.

# Should My Partner and I Break Up?

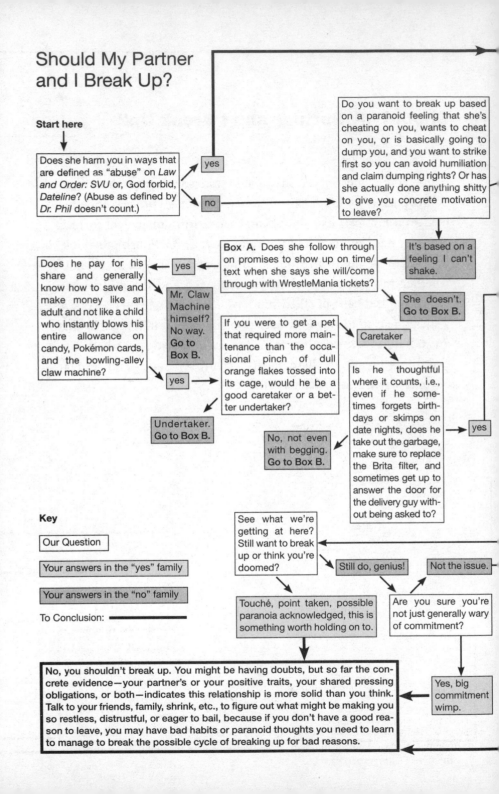

**Start here**

Does she harm you in ways that are defined as "abuse" on *Law and Order: SVU* or, God forbid, *Dateline*? (Abuse as defined by *Dr. Phil* doesn't count.)

yes

no

Do you want to break up based on a paranoid feeling that she's cheating on you, wants to cheat on you, or is basically going to dump you, and you want to strike first so you can avoid humiliation and claim dumping rights? Or has she actually done anything shitty to give you concrete motivation to leave?

It's based on a feeling I can't shake.

**Box A.** Does she follow through on promises to show up on time/text when she says she will/come through with WrestleMania tickets?

She doesn't. Go to Box B.

Does he pay for his share and generally know how to save and make money like an adult and not like a child who instantly blows his entire allowance on candy, Pokémon cards, and the bowling-alley claw machine?

yes

Mr. Claw Machine himself? No way. Go to Box B.

yes

If you were to get a pet that required more maintenance than the occasional pinch of dull orange flakes tossed into its cage, would he be a good caretaker or a better undertaker?

Caretaker

Undertaker. Go to Box B.

No, not even with begging. Go to Box B.

Is he thoughtful where it counts, i.e., even if he sometimes forgets birthdays or skimps on date nights, does he take out the garbage, make sure to replace the Brita filter, and sometimes get up to answer the door for the delivery guy without being asked to?

yes

**Key**

| Our Question |

| Your answers in the "yes" family |

| Your answers in the "no" family |

To Conclusion: ——————

See what we're getting at here? Still want to break up or think you're doomed?

Still do, genius!

Not the issue.

Touché, point taken, possible paranoia acknowledged, this is something worth holding on to.

Are you sure you're not just generally wary of commitment?

Yes, big commitment wimp.

**No, you shouldn't break up.** You might be having doubts, but so far the concrete evidence—your partner's or your positive traits, your shared pressing obligations, or both—indicates this relationship is more solid than you think. Talk to your friends, family, shrink, etc., to figure out what might be making you so restless, distrustful, or eager to bail, because if you don't have a good reason to leave, you may have bad habits or paranoid thoughts you need to learn to manage to break the possible cycle of breaking up for bad reasons.

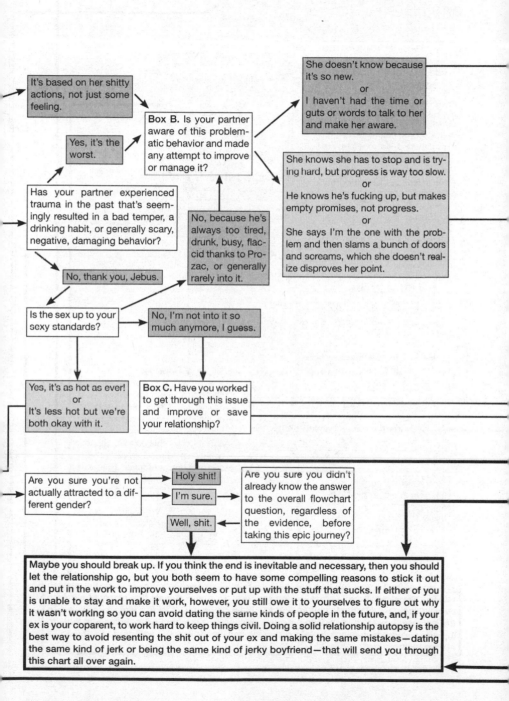

It's based on her shitty actions, not just some feeling.

Yes, it's the worst.

**Box B.** Is your partner aware of this problematic behavior and made any attempt to improve or manage it?

She doesn't know because it's so new.
or
I haven't had the time or guts or words to talk to her and make her aware.

She knows she has to stop and is trying hard, but progress is way too slow.
or
He knows he's fucking up, but makes empty promises, not progress.
or
She says I'm the one with the problem and then slams a bunch of doors and screams, which she doesn't realize disproves her point.

Has your partner experienced trauma in the past that's seemingly resulted in a bad temper, a drinking habit, or generally scary, negative, damaging behavior?

No, because he's always too tired, drunk, busy, flaccid thanks to Prozac, or generally rarely into it.

No, thank you, Jebus.

Is the sex up to your sexy standards?

No, I'm not into it so much anymore, I guess.

Yes, it's as hot as ever!
or
It's less hot but we're both okay with it.

**Box C.** Have you worked to get through this issue and improve or save your relationship?

Are you sure you're not actually attracted to a different gender?

Holy shit!

I'm sure.

Well, shit.

Are you sure you didn't already know the answer to the overall flowchart question, regardless of the evidence, before taking this epic journey?

Maybe you should break up. If you think the end is inevitable and necessary, then you should let the relationship go, but you both seem to have some compelling reasons to stick it out and put in the work to improve yourselves or put up with the stuff that sucks. If either of you is unable to stay and make it work, however, you still owe it to yourselves to figure out why it wasn't working so you can avoid dating the same kinds of people in the future, and, if your ex is your coparent, to work hard to keep things civil. Doing a solid relationship autopsy is the best way to avoid resenting the shit out of your ex and making the same mistakes—dating the same kind of jerk or being the same kind of jerky boyfriend—that will send you through this chart all over again.

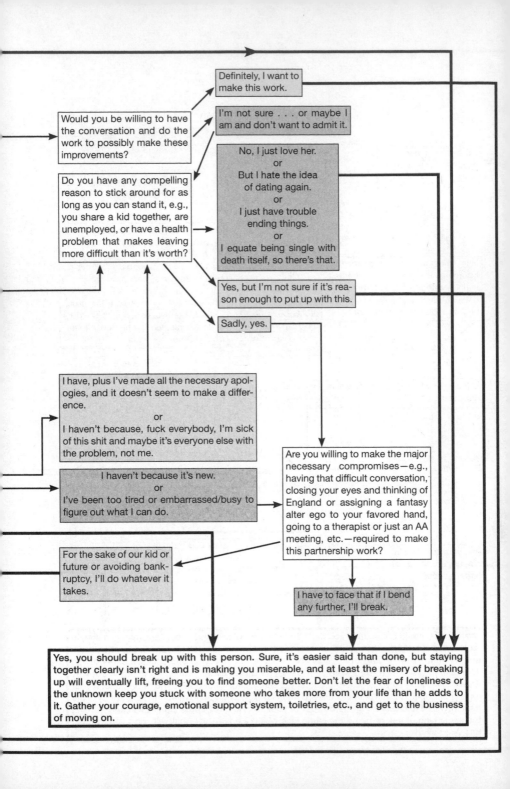

Would you be willing to have the conversation and do the work to possibly make these improvements?

Definitely, I want to make this work.

I'm not sure . . . or maybe I am and don't want to admit it.

Do you have any compelling reason to stick around for as long as you can stand it, e.g., you share a kid together, are unemployed, or have a health problem that makes leaving more difficult than it's worth?

No, I just love her.
or
But I hate the idea of dating again.
or
I just have trouble ending things.
or
I equate being single with death itself, so there's that.

Yes, but I'm not sure if it's reason enough to put up with this.

Sadly, yes.

I have, plus I've made all the necessary apologies, and it doesn't seem to make a difference.
or
I haven't because, fuck everybody, I'm sick of this shit and maybe it's everyone else with the problem, not me.

I haven't because it's new.
or
I've been too tired or embarrassed/busy to figure out what I can do.

Are you willing to make the major necessary compromises—e.g., having that difficult conversation, closing your eyes and thinking of England or assigning a fantasy alter ego to your favored hand, going to a therapist or just an AA meeting, etc.—required to make this partnership work?

For the sake of our kid or future or avoiding bankruptcy, I'll do whatever it takes.

I have to face that if I bend any further, I'll break.

Yes, you should break up with this person. Sure, it's easier said than done, but staying together clearly isn't right and is making you miserable, and at least the misery of breaking up will eventually lift, freeing you to find someone better. Don't let the fear of loneliness or the unknown keep you stuck with someone who takes more from your life than he adds to it. Gather your courage, emotional support system, toiletries, etc., and get to the business of moving on.

# Chapter 7

# F*ck Intelligence

Even those whose knowledge of dating is about as limited as a caveman's know that brains can be as important an asset in a partner as beauty. Mostly, however, people know that beauty won't help you solve problems, keep your shit together, or even learn how to read—you need intelligence for that, a fact that even the totally superficial (or Stone Age) can appreciate. Assessing the overall value of intelligence in a partner or its impact on a partnership, however, requires a little more mental capacity than your average knuckledragger may possess.

Being with someone smart has obvious benefits, especially if a partner's particular intelligence complements your weaknesses and helps you manage a part of your life that is otherwise difficult for you to handle on your own; if you're bad with people and your partner's a social whiz, or if you're bad with numbers and your partner's a CPA, then you have much to gain from getting together. So does she, assuming you have your own complementary strengths to contribute.

Unusual intelligence, on the other hand, creates expectations of accomplishment that are often a burden. For all the distinction, praise, and good grades it may bring early in life, it does not necessarily promise meaningful, enjoyable employment or good conversation. A person may be overcompetent at getting A's without developing a preference or calling, because when you're good at everything, you don't have to be passionate about anything to succeed. That can make for someone who, despite being brilliant, is totally boring, unfocused, and uncommitted.

While some kinds of intelligence are obvious (and may be overrated), others are less obvious than most people think and are easily underappreciated. Because intelligence comes in many different forms, people who are bright in one way are often less intelligent in others, and some kinds of intelligence are seldom reflected in academic achievement or recognized as intelligence at all. Those with people sense, common sense, and moral sense may not have advanced degrees, but their particular aptitude will have a huge effect on their ability to perform many jobs as well as manage a family and be a good partner. That's why evaluating a possible partner's abilities in these areas is critical, and why it's important to never assume that other, showier kinds of intelligence are more important.

You may also be tempted to assume that intelligent people who haven't accomplished much suffer from a lack of confidence or a character flaw that causes them to underachieve. That assumption, however, is based on the false notion that intelligence plus hard work always equals success. If you've ever worked for the boss's idiot cousin, followed national politics, or been a woman, you know that's not the case. In addition to bad luck, achievement can also easily be thwarted by subtle weaknesses in the way the brain processes information, particularly when it requires prolonged mental focus, effective executive function, or other specific cognitive skills.

So, instead of assuming that underachievement reflects bad attitude, pay attention to the fit between a person's intelligence and the kind of work they have to do to decide whether their attitude is causing poor performance or vice versa. Those who are truly smart know their areas of stupidity; those that don't tend to overrate the value of their intelligence and sometimes to be overrated for it.

There's nothing wrong with being attracted by intelligence, but if you are, don't overvalue it as an asset in a potential partnership or fail to evaluate its risks and benefits realistically. Intelligence can help someone make a good living, be a good communicator, and be a good parent, but it's just as likely to make someone bad at any or all of those functions. The only thing intelligence can guarantee in a partner is minimal literacy; after that, all bets are off.

So, before making assumptions about intelligence, think hard about what other abilities your partner will need for the partnership job description. Then sit back and watch that intelligence in action—what it does, not what it is—before deciding whether someone's far more capable than the caveman you made the person out to be, and whether the person's particular kind of intelligence will help your partnership or dumb it down.

### The Good Things You Want Intelligence to Deliver

- A companion who's so smart that she makes you feel as smart as you always wished to be by making you a willing participant in the kind of intellectual conversations that used to bore you to death.
- A sidekick whose brains will be your secret weapon in any debate, argument, or bar trivia night when your own mind comes up short.
- A sense of excitement, not dread, when you imagine what you

will hear at your future offsprings' parent-teacher conferences.

- A guarantee that your partner will always have a choice of good jobs that don't require driving, lifting, or asking if someone wants to add a drink and make it a value meal.
- An endless supply of thoughtful responses and clever solutions to the work and family problems that you find most bewildering.

**Profile of the Brainy**

Here is a list of traits associated with someone intelligent:

- *Physical attributes:* Piercing eyes (sharpened either through glasses or LASIK surgery), terrible posture (from reading, sitting at a computer, or doing both while also trying to be inconspicuous at a coffee shop so he doesn't get kicked out for taking up a table for too long), may dress more functionally than fashionably, and may have a gait and general manner that's only slightly less clumsy and absentminded than a newborn foal's.
- *Common occupations:* Getting yet another graduate degree, getting tenure, completing the *New York Times* Sunday crossword, consulting, researching, and generally doing jobs that are hard to label or explain.
- *What attracts you first:* The opportunity to have a smart conversation about something you're interested in, to learn something you didn't already know, to hear something cleverly put, or to watch someone who's confident about managing a situation that would leave you frozen and slack-jawed.
- *Red flags:* Noticing that socially appropriate things that should be said aren't while smart things are being said but at the wrong time and place, not being able to identify a single recent

instance of multitasking, struggling to find any prior relationship that survived the conflict with work, finding important tasks undone because the amount of thinking far surpasses the amount of actual doing, discovering that once-informative conversations have turned terse and patronizing.

## Seeking Intelligence

Intelligence isn't hard to identify, or at least, the lack of intelligence is as easy to identify as a misspelled neck tattoo and a car-window decal of Calvin peeing. Even so, it's much harder to find someone with the exact kind of intelligence that meshes nicely with yours, because intelligence alone is not a good guarantee of compatibility or the ability to work well together. So by all means, add intelligence to your list of desirable attributes, but be aware that it provides no shortcut to your procedures for identifying the character traits and functional attributes of the person you're seeking as a partner. If you're going to look for someone who's smart, be smart about how you go about it.

Here are three examples:

- *My boyfriend is smart, which I like and admire, but sometimes he talks down to me because I didn't go to college, and he can be condescending. I'm smart enough, but I don't have a lot of confidence (or advanced degrees like him, as he loves to point out), and his achievements sometimes intimidate me. My goal is to find the confidence to answer back when he gets snobby and nasty.*

- *I like to date smart girls, which is easy since, lucky for me, I work in a field that requires a great deal of intelligence. The unlucky part is that my job is also competitive, so whenever I date someone who's in my field, we tend to worry about who's more skilled or more likely to be promoted, and things get ugly. My goal is to find someone smart who doesn't care about who's the smartest.*

- *I wish I wanted to date smarter girls, but if I'm being honest, I'm much more attracted by women who aren't that bright. The problem is that, as much as I'm into them, the attraction is always short-lived because they don't make interesting partners in the long term. My goal is to figure out how to find smart women hot so I can have a relationship that lasts longer than two weeks and is enjoyable with our clothes on.*

Like so many apparent antitheses, intelligence and looks actually have a lot in common; people who seek them don't just tend to overvalue those qualities in others, but to feel insecure about those qualities in themselves. So, while you may pride yourself on seeking smarts over sexiness, overvaluing either may express more about what you think about yourself than what you desire in a partner. On the other hand, while dating a beauty will probably only teach you about the Paleo diet and CrossFit, dating a brain will teach you far more about yourself, namely the complex way that intelligence shapes what you have to offer to and gain from others.

Dating someone superintelligent will make you smarter, at least when it comes to learning the role that intelligence plays in a relationship and gaining a stronger sense of your own mental strengths and weaknesses. Getting the genius girlfriend of your dreams may bring your notions about intelligence down to earth (and if you're unlucky, it may be with a hard thud).

When you date someone smart, you learn the most from the experience by observing how you respond to the way a person's intelligence does or doesn't enhance her character and sense of humor and your way of interacting with each other. As usual, once that chemistry asserts itself, it does not necessarily turn out the way you wish and your influence over it may be limited.

If you have a better-educated boyfriend who sometimes gets snobby and nasty, it's understandable that your lack of education would undermine your confidence and tie your tongue. You might hope for a therapeutic intervention, heretofore-hidden savant status, or a bite from a radioactive genius or some other affirming or brain-building experience that improves your self-esteem and hands you the words to put him in his place. Unfortunately, self-doubting people tend to remain self-doubting, even after they're well educated, just as snobby people stay snobby when they're not educated at all (call it Cliff Clavin syndrome).

Instead of looking for a way to retaliate when he steps out of line, ask yourself whether his various assets (the good times, his reliability, his ability to do his share and act respectfully most of the time) outweigh his nasty moments. If not, your goal isn't to put him down, but to put him aside and move on; even he would agree that leaving a mediocre partner who constantly insults your intelligence is the smart thing to do.

Should you decide he's a keeper, at least provisionally, then offer him your observations and recommendations about his snotty side at a time when you aren't feeling angry or small. Don't feel compelled to argue or give details to prove your point; it's simply your opinion that he sometimes acts condescendingly and talks down to people and he should try to stop. If he doesn't agree that this is a problem, he should ask others whether they've observed it. React to his future bouts of snottiness by withdrawing from conversation and resuming only when his mucous attitude is under control.

If you find yourself both attracted to and competitive with smart women, you will have trouble developing a good partnership. Once competition starts, it's hard to tell who started it, so it's natural that you should wish to find someone who shares your interests and intelligence but isn't competitive with you. You might even yearn for the good old days when women knew how not to compete, but you'll be hard-pressed to find a smart woman who yearns to do anything with a guy like that but punch him in the dick.

Instead, do your best to get your competitive nature under control and reduce your combative behavior in a possible partnership. It would be nice if competitiveness were just a symptom of insecurity and easy to control and even erase as you become more confident professionally and personally. Unfortunately, if that were the case, it would probably already have improved after one or two relationships, and you wouldn't find yourself losing relationship after relationship by trying to win each battle of the wits.

Since competitiveness is more likely to occur when you and your partner both share the same type of intelligence and apply it in similar ways, your best bet for controlling the competitive element is to look for dates who are less like you. That's not to say you should look for women who aren't smart, just who aren't your particular type of smart or don't use their smarts the same way you do. Yes, it may be harder to talk to someone who isn't familiar with your work or fluent in its language. But if you branch out and date people with less familiar types of intelligence, you may well find people with whom you create sparks without kindling those old competitive fires that have traditionally left you feeling burned.

Guys who prefer women they don't intellectually respect are probably not that unusual; a guy's sex drive has its own weird way of responding to anxiety, so he may feel more sexually aroused by someone he doesn't care about or doesn't feel threatened or intimidated by than by someone whose opinion and affection matter.

Guys might hope to gain the confidence required to feel more sexually attracted to, or even brave enough to get within ten feet of, intelligent women; smart ladies are better at seeing guys' faults, making jokes at their expense, and leaving them for being such schmucks. Unfortunately, probably no therapist, pill, or shiny sports car has the power to make that confidence happen. In addition, if you value hot sex more than a respectful relationship, then you really are a schmuck, and stupid as well, which bodes ill for your relationship future. So, instead of waiting for a confidence boost, learn to accept that the strength of your sexual desire is clearly a bad criterion for partnership.

Obviously, some desire is necessary, but so is a partner who can do her share, be a good parent, and keep you in line when you're about to do something stupid. You're smarter if you rate a partner by the qualities that will make her a good partner rather than by those qualities that give you a constant boner. If you're ready to downgrade the importance of hot sex, credit yourself for being a smarter guy than many and for having a better chance of finding a partnership that will last.

Intelligence is well worth seeking in a partner, but it's foolish to overvalue, not just because of the drawbacks, but because it doesn't exist as a single, isolated asset. You learn about it by observing how your partner's intelligence meshes with your own and affects the way you solve problems together without letting his smarts distract you from evaluating his work ethic, commitment, and values. Then you can be sure your search for an intelligent partner won't get in the way of your dating intelligently.

*Quiz: Cranium Questionnaire—How smart are your
expectations for intelligence?*

1. After a few months together, your new boyfriend introduces
   you to his old college friends at a bar, and one of them mentions
   offhandedly that your boyfriend never actually graduated from
   their (sort of) alma mater. Later, you ask your boyfriend:
   A: Whether he has any plans to finish college or if he's content
      to live as a dummy/a liar/a single person without you.
   B: If he can still milk the alumni network for all that it's worth,
      because degrees are stupid and book learnin's overrated.
   C: About his reasons for dropping out, looking particularly
      for those related to drug use, commitment phobia, or law
      enforcement, as well as what he thinks he learned from the
      experience.

2. You go off to your girlfriend about how one of your favorite
   books, a classic novel that's a staple of any well-rounded library,
   is about to be violated/ruined by a film adaptation to star and be
   directed by Khloe Kardashian. When your girlfriend finally gets
   a word in, she reveals she's never heard of this book, which kind
   of blows your mind. Your reaction is to:
   A: Mention the names Tolstoy, Eliot, and Woolf, ask her what
      she thinks of them, and dump her if she can't present a cogent
      and original thesis about each.
   B: Allow her to fill you in on the Komplete Kardashian story,
      about which she could write a dissertation, which is impres-
      sive enough.
   C: Ask her what she likes reading and, if she's not a reader, find
      out what TV shows and movies she likes and why.

3. It turns out that the cute girl you've been flirting with in your running group who's so smart about stretches, ligaments, and avoiding injury isn't just up on exercise or a personal trainer, she's an actual MD/orthopedic surgeon. At your next group run, you:

   A: Are so impressed with her accomplishments and intellect that you can't think of anything to say to her except to ask her about the pain in your groin.

   B: Aren't particularly impressed, because she might be an MD but she's got a hitch in her stride and ho-hum times that will always prevent her from being a serious marathoner.

   C: Express interest in her work and ask her what she likes best about what she does and what ACL surgery is really like.

4. You meet a sweet, interesting guy at your friend's party, but his texts and emails are so full of typos, unreadable, and beyond what's acceptable even in the digital realm—he uses five commas in a row but never any emojis—that they're either written by a dog or it's possible that the guy can't read or write. You decide to:

   A: Find out how he ever managed to finish second grade and make it clear you don't date idiots (or dogs).

   B: Avoid written communication, suggest some literacy classes, and enjoy spending time together while reading billboards, menus, and road signs out loud for him.

   C: Find out more about his work and see if he's intelligent in other ways, such as at managing difficult situations and problem solving, even if he can't easily put his thoughts into writing (or small Japanese images).

5. You've always toyed with the idea of getting a specific master's degree so you could qualify for better jobs in your field, but

your new boyfriend with the PhD seems fixated on your going through with it, not for the better employment opportunities but so you can get closer to his supreme academic level. Your impulse is to:

A: Find out what kind of a master's degree would most impress him and start taking GRE classes and rounding up recommendations ASAP.

B: Just get two low-level jobs rather than have to crack a book again, so you learn to ignore his ivory-tower encouragement.

C: Tell him you appreciate his enthusiasm but that you won't be going back to school until you find just the right program at the right time, not to impress people by getting an advanced degree that you may not need and can't easily afford.

6. You're interested in a woman at work who's kind and fun to be around outside the office, but she's not that great to work with directly as her ideas are usually weak and it takes forever to explain projects to her (which she screws up, anyway). You decide to:

A: Take her out to lunch and ask her detailed questions about her work, education, and some basic algebra problems to see if she's more competent than she appears to be.

B: Ignore her workplace shortcomings because she comes through at beer pong and Nickelback karaoke at Thursday happy hour, and that's far more important.

C: Find time to talk with her about family, friends, and her life outside the office, which may show you where her hidden strengths lie and whether any of those strengths complement your weaknesses.

If you answered mostly A's . . .

You're so impressed with fancy degrees and a polysyllabic vocabulary that you've developed a bit of Mensa myopia; you can't see the dating potential in anyone who isn't potentially a genius. Perhaps experience hasn't yet taught you that smart people can be assholes just as easily as not-so-smart people, but as much as you love education, that's one lesson it's best to avoid learning yourself, particularly if it takes a bad marriage or just a major heartbreak to do it. Instead, push yourself to consider dating people who aren't academically gifted but may be great or gifted in other ways.

If you answered mostly B's . . .

You're much more interested in a person's ability to give you a good time than in his or her ability to solve problems and think clearly. While not-so-smart people are often better at having too much fun, marriage isn't fun, and if you're looking for something serious, then you have to look for people who care less about having a party going on and are more likely to have something going on in their brains.

If you answered mostly C's . . .

You're an adult who knows that a good partner with a good head on her shoulders won't just make life easier, but will make you smarter and more capable. Even as you're looking for someone intelligent, you're also aware that smarts come in many different flavors, so what's most important isn't to find the biggest brain, but the best complement to your own, so you can make up for each other's blind spots and broaden the number of things you can do well as a team.

## Did You Know . . . What the "Social Fake" Is?

You should, if you're book smart but socially stupid.

It's well-known that some people with advanced academic-style intelligence can fall short when it comes to learning social competence. TV is so fond of smart-and-socially-clueless protagonists that "rude Asperger's-y genius" has surpassed "brilliant doctor who's built like an American ninja warrior" and "bad-boy lawyer with great man hair" as the most common TV archetype.

In real life, people with advanced minds and substandard social skills aren't actually rude, they're just less capable of reading social cues; they can master the languages of science, math, and engineering, but body language and nuanced or abstract language aren't things they intuitively understand. They aren't ignoring your signals or accepted rules of social conduct; they just don't perceive them in the first place.

Of the many concepts taught by therapists who work with those on the autism spectrum, "the social fake," a concept introduced by speech and language therapist Michelle Garcia-Winner, is one that's useful for nerdy and awkward types overall, regardless of spectrum status. "The social fake" refers to adopting the kind of social customs that make no sense to someone with Asperger's, such as greeting random people by asking, "Hi, how are you?" or "Nice weather we're having, no?" and all the other bullshitty questions that are part of polite conversation.

What most people on the spectrum will tell you is that they don't ask such questions because it seems meaningless to acquire random information about random people. What therapists try to explain to them is that you're not asking to gain knowledge, but because it makes them feel comfortable and is considered good manners—it's a *social fake*, after all. The other person's answer ("Fine, thanks, beautiful day!") is often just as vacuous, so expectations of the exchange are mutual.

If you're not technically on the spectrum but find it easier to work with computers or dough or words all day than to make eye contact and social chitchat with the opposite sex, the social fake is easy enough to master, and unbelievably helpful. Just don't tell anyone who works in TV development, because if their rude-genius archetypes start learning social skills, they'll have to find a new trope to milk to death.

## Having Intelligence

When we're kids, being intelligent can either feel like a cross to bear or an excuse to put crosshairs on someone else; hunting season on nerds begins early in grade school and usually doesn't end until high school graduation. As you reach adulthood, however, intelligence starts to pay off, helping you achieve well-paying jobs, impress the opposite sex, or just keep yourself from losing fingers on the Fourth of July. Unfortunately, intelligence may still complicate the way people feel about you and what they expect from you, even though those expectations can now be too high and no longer inspire wedgies. Overrating intelligence in others or in yourself will distort your understanding of relationships and your own strengths and weaknesses. It may also shape your tastes and values in ways that make you pickier, harder to please, and less compatible with would-be friends. It's your job to learn how to manage it—as asset, liability, or both—as you seek a good partnership instead of a way to survive lunch period.

Here are three examples:

- *I'm one of those rare women in a STEM field of academia (science, technology, engineering, and math), so meeting guys is*

*unusually challenging. Dating within my field is looked down
upon because then I'll be seen as sleeping my way to the top or
as stealing credit from my other half. If I try to date outside the
sciences or academia, however, I tend to be too nerdy for most and
intimidate smart guys because I know more than they do about
"male subjects," i.e., math and science. I don't want to play dumb
to meet guys, but I don't know how to meet guys if I don't. My goal
is to find a partner who isn't intimidated by my brain.*

- *I'm smart, but not about people—I assume I'm somewhere on
the autism spectrum, but I've never bothered to get it checked
out—so I have trouble dating. I have a head full of stuff to talk
about and ideas that interest me, but I don't know how to make
small talk or read facial expressions to tell whether people are
interested, bored, or want to get away once I open my mouth. My
goal is to find someone I can talk to and figure out how to have a
relationship.*

- *Because I'm blond and fairly petite, guys tend to approach me as
if I were a slut and talk to me as if I were an idiot. I'm a respected
oncologist, so being treated like a dumb sorority girl is never not
infuriating. When guys aren't talking down to me, they're offended
because they think I'm talking down to them! My goal is to find
someone who can respect me for my mind, not just judge me by
my looks.*

To paraphrase a line from the movie *Bull Durham*, the world is
made for people who aren't cursed with self-awareness. That explains
why, in the dating world, intelligence and the self-awareness that
come with it often make the difficult job of finding someone even

harder. In many ways intelligence can be more monkey wrench than asset in finding a good relationship, particularly if imagination, fear, and expectation distort its impact.

Unlike the truly oblivious who glide through life in a magic cloud of stupid dust, smart people can't help but perceive, judge, and analyze far too much. That can make it harder to get and stay close to people, or for people to get close to you, or to deal with bullshit in general. As *Bull Durham* shows us, that's why the idiot gets unlimited girls and success in the major leagues while the smart guy rides the bus in pleated khakis. That's also why it's your job to assess the impact of intelligence realistically, in your dating experience and in your relationships with others.

For those whose intelligence intimidates prospective partners, disowning or hiding your intelligence is no answer. When you see how much easier it is for less intelligent friends to find a partner, it's natural to want to hide, disown, or even resent your gift, especially when it arouses envy or snide remarks. However, dumbing yourself down isn't a smart move; it will only end up harming your personality, and relationships, while easier to find, will be built on a big stupid lie. You'll wind up angry at those who can't accept the way you are and angry at yourself for making career and other sacrifices for the sake of other people's feelings.

Instead, accept that your intelligence, which is a gift in so many other ways, may make finding a good partner harder. Prepare to be patient and build your independence because it's better to be single than take on a doomed relationship by dating someone you know isn't worthwhile.

Use your pesky intelligence to widen your search and identify qualities and backgrounds that improve your compatibility odds. You're unlikely to find someone if you're feeling discouraged or have committed your time to a bad compromise, but if you're being your-self, making the best of your gift, and refusing to get close to anyone who isn't comfortable with the way you are, then your patience and smart sacrifice are likely to be rewarded.

If your intelligence comes as part of an Asperger's package, your relationships will require extra effort. It may be just as well that your personality doesn't give you the ability to fake your intelligence or act more conventionally, because there's a lot to be said for being a genuine person, especially when you're trying to make a meaning-ful connection. Unlike many people who find relationships diffi-cult, you've decided that they are nevertheless worth pursuing, even if doing so sometimes leaves you feeling helpless and humiliated. Having a positive attitude will go a long way toward taking the sting out of what can often be a negative experience.

Get coaching in the basics of emotional communication; some speech and occupational therapists specialize in teaching those on the spectrum how to navigate small talk, read facial expressions and body language, and create social situations that are comfortable. If you're unable to find a therapist, don't hesitate to ask a friend or family member what you could say to make a social situation easier, or what you said wrong if it caused people to withdraw. Think care-fully about what you wish to share in a partnership and what quali-ties you're looking for in a companion.

Sometimes, having to keep things simple and deliberate as you work on building the basics of a relationship will save you from making the mistakes that socially gifted people commonly do, such as getting carried away by flirting, flattery, or sexual chemis-try. In the end, you may do better than those who have an intuitive gift for relationships but have never had to think carefully about what they should stay away from. In the beginning, however, you need to study social skills and brace yourself for a steep learning curve.

Those who are both intelligent and blond may have to fend off a double set of stereotyped expectations. Again, a double gift can also bear a double curse. If you rail against the stupidity of guys who can't see beyond stereotypes, you don't improve your chances and may seem like a snob. And for good reasons you should not try to dumb down your speech, uglify your looks, or settle for the kind of guys who wish you'd do either.

Accept that, contrary to conventional expectations, your search is not going to be easy and it isn't your fault; it's just your bad excellent luck. Be patient, widen your search, and make it clear, up front, that you're smart and you look the way you look. You're looking for someone who is a good fit, which means a good guy who's confident enough to feel like your equal. You'll know it when you see it (and have a conversation with it), and you won't compromise until you do.

Whatever the gifts it bestows, intelligence can make many things, from finding a relationship to playing professional baseball, a lot more difficult. Don't ever conclude that you're misusing your gift or give up the search because you're bitter about the unfair response of others. As you're well aware, smart people are rare, so finding someone who can match your brains will require patience. Assess your needs, even if they're hard to meet, and keep searching while accepting that, even if the world makes it hard for people such as you, you will use your intelligence to find someone you can make a life with.

## Averaging Your Intelligence

Whether you think you're blessed with the highest intelligence or proudly scorn know-it-alls (or just know-more-than-nothings), here are some useful dos and don'ts when you're trying to impress, not alienate, the opposite sex.

| Smartness Snob | | Unashamed Ignoramus | |
| --- | --- | --- | --- |
| Do | Don't | Do | Don't |
| . . . be open to watching films that don't involve corsets or subtitles or aren't documentaries that make most people want to kill themselves. | . . . show open distain for comedic films whose humor is even more crass than that found on NPR's *Wait Wait . . . Don't Tell Me!* | . . . be polite when someone tries to sell you on an epic foreign novel they think you'd enjoy. | . . . respond by describing, in detail, the plot to every film in *The Expendables* franchise. |
| . . . allow yourself to consider that some recent TV dramas may be as well written and interesting as a good book (or at least a good novella). | . . . dry-heave when you realize that your date mostly enjoys the kind of books they sell in Target (not that you've ever shopped there, or you'd *actually* vomit). | . . . try to appreciate your date's enthusiasm when she excitedly explains an article she read about a new medical breakthrough that pertains to her research. | . . . try to impress said date by describing your own "medical condition," "shoulder shits," which you illustrate by showering her with armpit farts. |
| . . . stay calm and think twice before abruptly ending a relationship with someone whose college degree turns out to be a BFA. | . . . get a BFA. Just a piece of general advice to anyone: it would be simpler just to set a pile of money on fire and go straight into a career as a lifelong disappointment. | . . . be open to going with a date to a lecture, literary event, or classical-music concert. | . . . push yourself to put up with a poetry reading, especially if it's open mic. No date is worth it. |

## Intelligence and Marriage

Even when you are settled in a marriage and know each other well, intellect can still cause trouble; just because you have a lot of intelligence *on* your spouse doesn't meant the effect of mental intelligence won't mess with your relationship. After a certain point, you or your partner's mental gifts are no longer as impressive or helpful as they once were, or they're more annoying than ever before. If you can't adjust your expectations to accommodate the new market for your mind, then your marriage is going to become a mess. Don't count intelligence a blessing until you assess its pressures, expectations, and how it could affect your marriage over time. You can learn as much as possible about your spouse, but gather intelligence early *about* intelligence and how it could impact your marriage in the long term.

Here are three examples:

- *My husband is amazingly gifted, but as I discovered after we started a family, he's also clueless about politics, his health, the way people feel, and the world outside his brain in general. He makes a good living and he's a decent guy, but it's hard to get him to take care of himself, and the older he gets, the more of an absentminded professor he becomes. My goal is to get him to be smart about the basics without fighting with him every time I need him to do what's normally considered the bare minimum.*

- *I like that my wife is smart and accomplished, but she can't seem to see that our son isn't like her—he's not stupid, but he's more creative and visual than book smart and disciplined, and either way, he's a nice kid whom any parent should be proud of. My wife can't see beyond his handful of mediocre grades, however, so she's*

*after him every day to work harder and push himself more, and
it causes endless conflict. My goal is to get my smart wife to be
smarter about her kid.*

- *My husband is the smart one in our family, and I'm grateful for
  that, but it has always intimidated me. We've got great kids, and
  I do interesting things, but he's the one who's made the big bucks,
  and I realize after all these years, I've always deferred to him even
  when I thought he was wrong. I think he could tolerate some
  disagreement. My goal is to find the courage to stand up to him
  when necessary, regardless of how much I'm intimidated by his
  intelligence.*

Marriage is inherently rife with high expectations, from believing that your spouse will one day remember to take the trash out and not expect it to walk to the curb by itself, to presuming you can stand to share a bed, bathroom, and, yes, beyond with this one person until your life (or at least *The Simpsons*) ends. The problem with living with intelligence in your marriage—be it your own or a partner's—is that it can create additional expectations that are intimidating and distracting.

After all, exceptional gifts require exceptional accomplishments, and while they occasionally happen and make you happy, they more often make you feel merely adequate and worried about what you have to accomplish next and whether you'll actually succeed. So don't forget the priorities in a long-term relationship that never change, such as being a decent person, doing your share, being a good partner. Intelligence can be fit into that framework, not vice versa.

If you are married to an "absentminded professor," it's understandable to find the absentmindedness more disturbing and irritating (like Jerry Lewis, "nutty" or no) than charming and amusing (like eighties Eddie Murphy, his "nutty" days a distant nightmare). To those who work with him, enjoy his conversation, and require nothing more than his outstanding work and ideas, such a professor type is a pleasure to know and his partner should count herself lucky. To the partner who keeps him fed, clothed, and out of trouble while getting no practical help in return, it's not so much fun and must often feel as if you've unfairly been promised a husband and wound up with an additional child instead.

You'd like to change the rules and find it hard to understand why someone so smart can be so dumb. If you had trained him from childhood, you might have been able to improve his habits of self-care, chores, and basic human interactions. Then again, your efforts might have failed because the absentminded-professor traits come not from poor parenting but potent genes that are too powerful to control.

After lowering your expectations, look for the important tasks you need help with that he'd realistically be able to take on; don't think of what's fair, but of what's possible. Then ask yourself whether that behavior can be incentivized simply, using your power to control household supplies, major purchases, and recreational activities. If you need ideas and inspiration, watch a TV show featuring an animal-training expert, from whisperer to hunter, and take copious notes.

Finally, present your plan positively. Let him know that you assume he wants to take care of his share but his attention span often defeats him, so you've identified some basic tasks he can do and some tricks for capturing his attention and helping him remember. Put the plan into effect, proclaiming he will feel better if he can improve his contributions at home, and discourage further, distracting discussion. You can't make an absent mind present, and resentment will probably drive it further into the mists wherein it dwells. What you can sometimes do is improve its management so it's less absent and more aware.

If being intelligent makes your wife intolerant of your nonintellectual son and his poor academic performance, it can be hard to watch her criticize him without trying to tell her to stop. Your powers are limited, and opposing her directly may just make her feel that you don't care about his education or value her efforts to help. If she can't see that she's doing more harm than good, find a positive way to credit her love and dedication while asking her to examine the negative effects of her actions. Your goal is to help her learn from experience without making her defensive, while simultaneously modeling a positive and supportive approach to your son.

To avoid possible miscommunication and a quarrel, try writing out your argument first. Begin by praising her commitment to trying to get your son to work hard and develop his mind, and assure her that you don't think she or your son has failed. She has just demonstrated that his mind doesn't respond well to school-based education and parental incentives, at least not yet.

Assure her that you share her standards and continue to hope that his intellectual gifts will develop as he gets older, but you will not be pushing him hard in the near future because such efforts have had a negative effect on his confidence and no positive effect on his learning. If she disagrees, tell her you're eager to get advice from teachers and other experts.

If all fails, you may need to separate to protect your son (although your living apart, assuming she has partial custody, may offer him less protection, not more). With luck, your wife will accept that her efforts aren't working through no fault of her own and credit your son with being a good kid despite the frustrations of not having her gifts. If not, you can hope that she will eventually agree with your observations and, until then, not feel she's lost your support.

Intelligence can be intimidating, even after you've known and lived with someone for years, particularly if you're a self-doubter and married to someone who isn't. Initially, perhaps you hoped your partner's certainty would rub off on you, but you realize it's now time to develop confidence of your own.

You might hope to boost your intellectual confidence with an intensive course in quantum theory (or perhaps just a course of psychotherapy). In reality, self-doubt tends to persist no matter how much you learn about the external or internal universe, so you will probably need to develop an ability to phrase independent opinions even when you don't feel particularly confident.

Begin by considering a current issue on which you and your partner disagree and which is important enough for you to take separate, independent action on if your partner's views don't change. Then, with the help of a friend or a therapist, research the issue as if you were preparing a judgment, and marshal your arguments. When the issue comes up again, be prepared to present your view, being careful not to express a need for him to agree.

Again, it often helps to write out your position, especially if your natural shyness tends to make you panic in confrontations so you forget what you want to say. Don't imply that he has stifled dissent or been unresponsive to your opinions, just state your own view, what you intend to do about it, and what you hope he will do about it. Then drop the subject without implying that you need him to agree or that you're incapable of thinking and acting independently. You may never feel fully confident when you're around your smart husband, but you can prevent your lack of confidence from interfering with your ability to say what needs to be said and acting independently when it's appropriate and necessary.

You can't help being intelligent and you probably can't change the way you and your partner feel about it. What you can do is make sure intelligence-stimulated attitudes and expectations don't make you stupid or intimidated, stop you from doing what you think is right, or add to the already-difficult goals of marriage so that they become impossible.

## Did You Know . . . Truth, or Bullshit?

*We examine widely accepted beliefs about relationships to determine whether they're true (or not so much). The phrase in question:*
"The heart wants what it wants."

This phrase, made famous by Woody Allen before starting a life with his stepdaughter, is often employed by men or women to explain and justify stupid romantic decisions. It's basically a way of taking the blame for leaving your husband for his brother, dumping the younger woman you left your first wife for, for an even younger woman, or, most pertinently to this chapter, exclusively dating pretty morons and passing the blame off from you to one of your organs. You didn't mean to ruin your life and those of everyone around you, but your heart made a compelling argument—namely "Gimme!"

Lots of other things also *want what they want*—toddlers, dogs, Tea Party congresspeople—but that doesn't mean they should always *get* what they want. If we can say no to them and their urge to fuck up our lives, even though they really want to play with that rusty knife, bark endlessly at the horse on TV, or bankrupt the world economy, you can as well refuse your heart's yearning to completely fuck up *your* life.

So let the heart want as much as its little self desires, but empower your brain to keep those yearnings in check so you can keep your life from going ass up.

VERDICT: SUCH UTTER BULLSHIT

Looking for a smart partner seems like the smart choice, but even intelligence can't outsmart the variety of complications that come with positive traits. The intelligence you really need is the smarts to see through each other's bullshit, know when the other guy is right, and know when to speak up and when to shut up. What you don't need is intelligence that glories in petty accomplishments or is good at fooling people, including each other. Even when the right kind of intelligence is part of the picture, you still need to be prepared to work harder to figure out whether your prospective partner is really the person he seems to be, and whether you'll actually get along when you're too tired, angry, or just overwhelmed to think straight, let alone near genius level.

| What to Look For | What to Achieve/What Not to Be Fooled By |
| --- | --- |
| Mutual attraction | . . . that may include the pleasures of the mind, but doesn't blind you to looking for actions that show character, commitment, and the ability to manage the parts of life that aren't pleasurable at all. |
| Mutual respect | . . . for the way you learn from and help each other make smart decisions, and not for the combined total of your IQs and advanced degrees. |
| Shared effort | . . . in giving and seeking intelligent advice and making smart decisions, rather than in impressing each other with who's right, more clever, and generally the smartest person in the room or marriage or world. |
| Common interests | . . . in each other's accomplishments, intelligent choices, and working through tough problems together, rather than in showy cleverness and intellectual dazzle. |
| Common goals | . . . to manage work and family in ways you wouldn't have been able to think of on your own, no matter how impressive or pedestrian your own intelligence may be. |

# Five Things to Consider before Deciding to Get a Divorce

1. *Prioritize safety:* If you think your partner is scary and mean, assess whether the risk of harm is real and immediate. If it is, it's your job to protect yourself ASAP, not first figure out why your spouse gets so angry or what you can say or do to reduce the tension. The time to analyze his or her behavior is later (if ever); getting out and staying safe is more important than staying to talk things over.

2. *List the essentials of a good-enough marriage:* Considering all the marriages you've ever observed closely, from your parents' to your old frat brother's with his mail-order bride, ask yourself which ones never had a chance or were unhealthy and why, e.g., one partner didn't do her share or was too quick to anger or only spoke Ukrainian. Then, if your marriage has one or more of those toxic qualities that make it substantially worse than living single, be realistic in considering whether your partner or you could make the changes necessary. Remember to distinguish between character, which doesn't change, and behavior, which does (occasionally) (if someone tries hard).

3. *Look at your decision through a business lens:* List the pros and cons of marriage and divorce, putting aside negative feelings and focusing on the line items of dissolving a partnership, i.e., figuring out how to survive the splitting of assets and responsibilities and the increase in personal expenses. Compare security, income, savings, lifestyle, and parenting, as well as what you may have to sacrifice by going solo or single income, such as your nice house or your show dog.

4. *Consider the logistics of leaving:* You can't give yourself a choice until you know what the choice will require and you can create and execute a realistic exit plan. If you think your partner's idea of a fair split of possessions, custody, or child care isn't likely to be the same as yours, then you need to know your state's legal guidelines, the conditions that would prompt a judge to make exceptions, and the cost of legal help. Hopefully, all you'll need is to find an affordable place to live that doesn't screw up your commute or your kids' school district. Never let fear prevent you from finding out what you need to do or to convince you that there's no way to do it.

5. *Explore therapy while acknowledging its limitations:* Sure, a therapist can help you understand and speak more positively to each other, but when your communication Sherpa isn't around, you'll both usually slip when you're under stress. Therapy may help you understand that what you don't like about your spouse is part of the way he is, and that he would be that way with anyone, no matter how great his love and caring; but it probably can't change him, leaving you to decide whether the marriage is worthwhile in spite of what you don't like. Ultimately, therapy can't change either of your personalities, but it may get you and your spouse to take your differences less personally, see what behavior needs to change, and assess whether such change (and staying together) is an actual possibility.

# Chapter 8
# F*ck Wealth

Unlike the other traits explored in this book, most people don't see "wealth" as a quality to seek in a partner. In pop music, money is usually seen as an impediment to true love—it can't buy love, it changes everything, it rules everything around you (at least in cash form)—as money supposedly represents greed, selfishness, and the desire to exploit what belongs to someone else. Looking for someone with wealth is seen as the mark of a mercenary character or a Jane Austen–era class snobbishness. Overall, wealth is seen as the wrong reason to marry someone unless you're eager to be lonely and unhappy in a big fancy house with a big empty heart.

In reality, wealth is a resource that is necessary for survival, raising families, and managing bad luck, and partnering with someone who depletes your resources or has little to offer is likely to undermine many of the goals that a partnership is supposed to advance. There's a difference between looking for someone rich and looking for someone resourceful, and the latter is the kind of wealth that every good partner should have.

That's because, once the novelty of romance fades, love thrives on a shared feeling that partnership makes life better than it would otherwise be, so if the partnership falters because one person can't make or save money and poverty hurts the kids, love is not likely to last. You can't continue to respect or value someone who isn't working as hard as you are or isn't exerting the same self-discipline and self-deprivation to advance and protect your family.

Even if women have advanced since the days of Austen and are now able to support themselves (at seventy-seven cents to a man's dollar, but still), it remains as true today as ever that you must acquire resources before you can afford a partnership, assuming that the goal of your partnership is a family. If you have no resources and no likelihood of getting them, having children will make you poor, guilty, and helpless. Before you begin a partnership, you need to consider how much wealth you will need and what the partnership is supposed to accomplish. Looking for wealth isn't about looking for a sugar daddy/mama, it's about looking for someone who can work with you to provide at least enough sugar to keep a family in the financial sweet spot.

Even more important than knowing the financial resources that someone brings to your partnership is rating the way he or she manages those resources. If someone has resources but spends recklessly and without prioritizing, you'll have trouble making joint decisions even if the money doesn't run out. You need a partner who manages money according to values you share.

In addition, watching how someone spends his money tells you more about his values than what he says about them, so you need to know if his money is where his mouth is, or somewhere else. How a person spends will also tell you much about his boundaries, i.e., his ability to care for others while remaining responsible for his own needs. Your prime concern is not how much money she lavishes on you but whether that spending reflects an ability to balance conflicting needs, such as those to save and also be generous, rather than reacting to a single impulse. Find someone who cannot just provide resources, but be prudent and responsible for the family's sake.

Don't apologize for knowing how much money you need and assessing how well a prospective partnership can contribute to your efforts. Being a good financial planner is not the same as being a gold digger; in examining a person's resources, you are not being greedy or ignoring the way you feel about her personality. Instead, you are assessing how she implements professed values and makes the difficult management decisions that a partnership obliges you to make together.

Money may be a destructive force, especially in romance, but not having it does a lot more damage than having just enough. Instead of limiting your search to those with offshore accounts or writing off wealth altogether as unimportant, stick to the middle ground and look for someone who's just plain accountable.

## The Good Things You Want Wealth to Deliver

- An end to worry, fear, envy, disrespect, impatience, and the deep sense of dread caused by the words "college loans" and "credit score."
- Awesome dates who are so blinded by your big spending that they can see past your oily appearance, dull conversation, and nonexistent manners and straight into your heart (and bank accounts).
- An end to any possible arguments about child care, dirty dishes, or dirty children thanks to your well-financed fleet of

nannies, cleaning ladies, nannies to take care of the cleaning ladies, etc.

- An end to hard choices when you care about three people in need but can afford to help no more than one, so you need never fail to appease anyone who would otherwise make you feel guilty, such as the two people who dropped dead because you couldn't afford to be there.
- The best doctors, personal trainers, private chefs, shrinks, and colonic artists so that you can feel healthy while never being denied anything (except dignity, if you're going with the colonics).

## Profile of the Provider

Here is a list of traits associated with someone of means:

- *Physical attributes:* The toned muscles, white teeth, and smooth skin of someone who invests a lot of time and effort in her looks, but the mussy hair and low-key-yet-expensive wardrobe of someone whose wealth is at a visual frequency that's only perceptible to other rich people.
- *Common occupations:* If not slaving away in a competitive field to achieve means (e.g., law, business, plastic surgery for internal organs), then she may have been born into wealth (or retired after a long career, or just selling an app that makes meow sounds) and working in philanthropy and sitting on various boards, be they of museums and hospitals or the foundation to fight bird cholera.
- *What attracts you first:* Her willingness to spoil you, let you cut the line with her, and generally give you entrée into the world of the 1 percent without your having to worry about the bill (so

triggering you to yearn forever for a lasting relationship that comes with a permanent membership in the VIP club of life).

- *Red flags:* An inability to say no and distinguish personal survival priorities, such as having rent money and avoiding debt, from less important needs, such as having hair-product money and never sleeping on sheets with less than a four-digit thread count; a yen for partying, drinking, and generally burning money, time, and brain cells; friendships based on status, fabulousness, or access to cocaine, rather than mutual support and shared responsibilities and values.

## Seeking Wealth

Dating a rich person seems like a great idea, particularly when you're bored, broke, and lonely and a new rich boyfriend would literally solve all your problems. Eventually, however, you realize that wealth also shapes the culture, expectations, and interactions of the people who do and don't have it, and having a money-messiah partner creates a whole new set of problems you never thought about and couldn't previously afford. Dating someone rich, or at least significantly richer than you, is almost like dating someone from another country, which means dealing with a different language and set of customs and manners. While that makes for wacky misunderstandings on sitcoms, it is a lot less fun in real life when the unavoidable class gap leads to confusion and hurt. That doesn't mean you should hate or avoid dating people who have more or less money than you, but you shouldn't expect a richer partner to improve your life, or for you to be the answer for someone with fewer funds. Being with someone whose wealth makes him or her hard to relate to can make you feel far more uncomfortable and lonely than being bored and broke ever did.

Here are three examples:

- *I don't resent my boyfriend's money, but he always gives me presents knowing that I can't reciprocate his generosity, and that makes me uncomfortable. When I try to refuse his presents or gently chide him for being too thoughtful, he gets defensive, hurt, and upset. We work together so well in every other way, I'd hate to see this one issue ruin our relationship. My goal is to find a way to have a comfortable, equal relationship with someone who is much richer than I am.*

- *Things have always been so easy for my girlfriend—she comes from money and has a trust fund, so she doesn't understand how to save or do without. I like her sophistication and the way she's comfortable wherever she goes, but she seems oblivious about money, so she sometimes says and does inappropriate things without having a clue she's offended anybody who's not also loaded. My goal is not to be prejudiced against her just because she is so privileged.*

- *I was always good at school and am the first person in my blue-collar, high-school-dropout family to go to college. Now, however, when among my peers who share my level of education and subsequent social class, I feel as if I don't belong. When I date college-educated women, they don't have a clue about where I come from and can be condescending and ignorant about it. My goal is to find someone who can accept my brain and my background.*

The ideal relationship dynamic is for partners' strengths and weaknesses to complement each other—in an area where one person struggles, the other excels, making them a dynamic duo of domesticity. The one area where this isn't always true, however, is money, because if one partner lacks wealth while the other is swimming in it, the contrast is not one of personal strengths, but of circumstances. A difference in wealth can interfere with a budding relationship by creating differences in expectations and assumed responsibilities.

For instance, receiving gifts that are far more costly than anything you can afford or reciprocate is like receiving any bad gift; what makes an expensive gift worse than just a bad one, such as a handmade iPhone sweater or anything with an "As Seen on TV!" label, is that it doesn't just make you feel bad about your relationship, it makes you feel guilty, broke, and bad about yourself. When the boyfriend who is trying to make you feel special discovers his overly rich gift has done the opposite and made you miserable, he may well feel hurt, creating conflict and making you both feel that you don't know each other at all.

You may wish he had the skill to find a perfect gift that makes you happy and costs almost nothing, but he's unlikely to be able to pull this off unless he has the smarts and wealth to pay for advice from a professional shopper. Besides, when you find out that he spent money to hire someone to figure out what you'd like, you'll be even more upset. So you're wiser to accept the unhappy way you feel about his wealth and instead review the overall quality of give-and-take in your relationship.

Don't be distracted by his generous gift because, if being generous with money is easy for him, it's no indicator of whether he'll be generous with things that count, such as with his time and effort, particularly when the job is unromantic. Instead, add up the giving qualities that matter most in the long run, such as whether he's a hard worker, a good and trustworthy friend, and willing to save as much as he spends and invest in the same things you do.

Just because your conscience requires financial parity in gift giving doesn't mean that your own contributions, in thoughtfulness and
investment, aren't equal to his. If you were judging the situation as a
friend would—as opposed to judging it through the lens of your own
financial shame and insecurity—you would value his giving according to the effort, sacrifice, and hard work he contributes and not by
the money he spends and would judge yourself according to what you
know and believe without the reflex guilt of an overactive conscience.

Once you're square with your own giving, you're free to accept
valuable gifts without feeling obliged to give an equivalent amount
in dollars and without overvaluing a person's generosity because of
his financial contributions. With luck, you can have your cake and
eat it by finding a rich guy who can also be a good partner (even if
his gift-giving skills are lacking).

Dating someone who has grown up so wealthy that she never
thinks about money can be fun, particularly if you enjoy her character, sense of style and confidence, can tolerate her ignorance about
the way other people live, and aren't generally choking on resentment and jealousy. You have to wonder, however, if her inexperi-
ence with saving and her obliviousness of the impact of careless
statements about money on others will change once your relationship allows you to give her constructive advice—or just straightfor-
ward observations—she may not have received before.

Ask her to consider how she would make tough resource decisions if necessary, and see if she can be more thoughtful about the
financial worries and concerns of others (being careful not to make
her defensive about her own wealth and circumstances). Watch to
see if she can assess her resources in terms of the cost of kids, their
education, and her long-term security. Ask yourself if she could
stop spending if she needed to or just for the sake of finding other
techniques for sustaining her sense of well-being. Look for her

willingness to have relationships with people who are less wealthy and to invest in the effort required.

She may overvalue the confidence that comes from disregarding money, especially if, as it does for so many, her wealth has become a comforting addiction. In that case, she may not be able to change this unfortunate character flaw so easily. Hopefully, she will be interested in freeing herself from the feel-good shortcuts of wealth and your relationship will be a positive step in that direction. If she isn't interested in considering how the less fabulous live, it's time to move on before your life together becomes unfabulous, indeed.

A special discomfort arises from hanging out with rich or even middle-class people if you've grown up blue-collar and poor. Even when you've thoroughly deserved scholarships and promotions and are well liked by the wealthy people in your new world, your hard-earned success may leave you feeling guilty, isolated, and disloyal to those you've left behind. Dating someone from your new world may deepen your feeling of being a stranger in a strange social class or, worse, of becoming the worst thing anyone from the old neighborhood can be: somebody who thinks he's better than everybody else.

It's natural to want to find someone in your new world who accepts you the way you are, or at least understands what you're going through, but that may be impossible. Even if someone who has never worried about money could fully understand your experience, she might well have trouble overcoming your nonacceptance of yourself.

So when you meet an educated woman who is interested in you and your background, don't let guilt oblige you to depend on her understanding. Instead, tell her proudly where you come from, allow her to connect the dots, and don't accept anyone who isn't impressed with what you've accomplished. You'll have a good chance of finding a partner if you look for the same qualities in her character that helped you to work hard and travel as far as you've come.

Don't judge yourself by the friendships that dissolve because of envy or your inability to bridge a growing gap between your past and future, or blame yourself because former friends reject you for seeming stuck-up or uncaring. Judge yourself by your effort and good heart, respect yourself for trying, and learn to bear the loneliness that can arise from your kind of success, where you feel that you can never go home again or feel totally at home in your new world.

Dating someone whose relationship and experience with money is different from yours generates doubts and problems that can't easily be erased. Stay focused on what a prospective partner does with money, rather than with how much she has, and you'll learn whether she has the basic qualities you're looking for. If she does, your money differences need not tip the balance between you, and the ideal relationship dynamic may still be in reach.

### Quiz: Cash Questionnaire—Is Your Date Too Financially Focused?

1. Your first date, at a moderately priced restaurant of your choosing, seems to have gone well—lots of lighthearted chitchat and laughs—but when the check arrives, your potential boyfriend does the following:

    A: He pulls out his strange credit card, which he explains is so exclusive to big spenders that it's made of pure gold, and insists that you two have your next date at one of the restaurants he's invested in (after going there in his private plane).

    B: He dumps three different cards out of his wallet and indicates his willingness to pay his share as soon as he figures out which one isn't maxed out.

    C: Offers to pay, but is happy to accept your offer to pay half if that would make you more comfortable, all while suggesting how much he looks forward to doing this again and getting to treat you next time.

2. On your third date with a girl you like, she's running late, so she asks you to meet her at her place before you go out to a movie, giving you a chance to look around her apartment. You notice:
   A: That her giant place in a superfancy neighborhood is filled with top-of-the-line appliances, artwork you swear you've seen in museums, and a coffee table covered with high-end-fashion and interior-design magazines that contain profiles of the apartment.
   B: That the location isn't safe, there's so much garbage in the living room that it may count as a fourth roommate, and that the pile of unpaid bills in the bathroom may count as the fifth.
   C: That it's neither a showplace nor a hovel, but an affordable, clean, homey apartment in a neighborhood she's not likely to get murdered in.

3. While getting to know a few facts about your new boyfriend, the topic of his exes comes up, and they all seem to share the same financial profile. Turns out he mostly dates girls who:
   A: Had eight homes, parents who donated buildings to the college they most wanted to go to, and sweet-sixteen/coming-out parties that cost more than the GDP of most African countries; all facts that your new boyfriend seems a little too proud of.
   B: Work at nonprofits or in social work, care a lot about recycling and rescuing cats that are missing at least one leg or eye, and were always there for him with a warm bed and a homemade organic meal when he was unemployed and broke (which was pretty much all the time).
   C: Were employed, independent, and savvy enough at budgeting to afford vacations, although you'd rather not see any

of the pictures of him in Belize with his old girlfriend in a
bikini, even if there's also a monkey in the shot.

4. When the Powerball prize approaches a billion dollars, you and
   your new girlfriend decide to buy a ticket for fun. When you ask
   her what she would do with the grand prize, she says:

   A: She would finally get that bigger yacht she's had her eye on,
      maybe buy her favorite shoe company so she'd have first dibs
      on the fall line, and see if she could buy some human organs
      on the black market just for fun.

   B: She'd "invest" most of it in buying *more* lottery tickets, but
      also give some to her brother once he gets out of jail so he can
      go to rehab (eighth time's the charm!) and maybe finally get
      into selling cosmetics door-to-door.

   C: She'd get the lump sum, pay off all her debts, buy a nice place
      to live that has good resale potential, and take her family to
      dinner at her father's favorite "special occasion" steak place
      before putting the rest into a rainy-day fund.

5. When you and your boyfriend decide to move in together, he
   agrees to move into your place since you own while he rents.
   When it comes to choosing between your furniture and his, his
   is fancier (which isn't surprising, considering his salary is much
   higher than yours), while yours is a mix of stuff inherited, bought
   at IKEA, found at antique stores, etc. He proposes:

   A: To throw out all of his furniture and yours and hire his abra-
      sive interior-designer friend whose hourly rate matches your
      rent to refurnish the whole place with the most expensive,
      design-forward items he can find (that you will always be
      afraid to sit on or touch).

   B: To keep his stuff, since he hasn't paid it all off yet, and replace all of your stuff with new furniture you'll buy on layaway, although you might have to do without a bed in the meantime, but it's worth sleeping on the floor and racking up credit-card debt if you can get a mattress with two sleep-number settings.

C: That you give him your ideas on long-term decorating, imply-ing that he's happy to invest more in your shared home (because he earns more) and generally invest in your relationship.

If you answered mostly A's . . .

Your date loves money so much, from the making of it to the spending of it, that he should probably be marrying it instead of dating you. If you've got it or are good at helping him play with it and revel in the respect it brings, you will have a good time together. If you need to be valued for your other attributes or don't see money as the pathway to happiness, fun, and personal validation, you will ultimately disappoint this person, and after too much grotesque extravagance he will quickly make you feel as if you need a shower.

If you answered mostly B's . . .

Your date doesn't care much about making or keeping money, but her sensibility is less monklike and more mooch-rific; to compensate for her inability to spend or save wisely, she's devel-oped a nonmaterialistic way of getting others to pay her bills. Stay with her and you're next in line to both manage and supple-ment her finances. Whatever you think you need to earn to sup-port yourself and your plans, double or triple it if you continue dating this person (or don't continue dating this person and just save up for professional matchmaking services instead).

If you answered mostly C's . . .

Your date values money at its market-relationship value,

without inflation; he sees it for what it can do in a practical sense, not for how it makes him feel or impresses dates such as you. He may never be a sugar daddy, but he'll also never be a leech, and most important, you'll be able to trust him to make smart financial decisions for your possible family. He cares less about spoiling you than contributing to a dream you can build together, and if you're more interested in building a family than being flashy, he's probably got his priorities straight.

### The Particulars of the 1 Percent: Pros and Cons of Dating Different Varieties of Rich People

While dating any rich person has the advantage of financial security, not every fortune is created equal; whether someone's finances are earned or inherited, nouveau or historical, can all impact his or her good and bad qualities as a potential mate. Here's a simple breakdown of a few different types of wealthy people and how their specific type of wealth can shape them as a partner.

|  | Pro | Con |
| --- | --- | --- |
| Secret trust fund | Often creative, using his wealth to underwrite a career in the arts or to start charities, and eager to disassociate himself from his wealth (as opposed to spending ostentatiously and making it rain in strip clubs) due to embarrassment, since, unlike the artists he runs with, he ain't starving. | Given his combination of financial security and shame, he can be terrible at managing money and appreciating his luck. May be aimless and bad at making important decisions due to the lack of motivation and experience making hard choices that needing to afford electricity can provide. |

| | Pro | Con |
|---|---|---|
| New money | Is willing to spend large sums on all the stuff she always wanted but could never before afford, not just so every day can feel like Christmas (if you have a tree under which you can fit pool tables and boats), but so she can keep up with the old-money crowd, not realizing said crowd is running away from her gauche behavior. | Having never been rich means having never learned how to save or invest money in bulk; even if business savvy is what got her rich, saving savvy is a different Learning Annex class altogether, so she's at risk for burning through her new fortune or just squandering it on Jet Skis and loans to cousins who need the start-up funds to open vape shops. |
| Old money | Can offer a window into a world that is foreign to at least 99.9 percent of the population, who've only seen it on PBS and in Brooks Brothers catalogs. Financial security can extend to guaranteed jobs in family-run businesses, to financial firms, to private islands off Massachusetts, etc. | Snobbishness abounds, so that window into his world is often only opened a crack to those whose money is newer or, gross, far less plentiful. Laziness and aimlessness also arise from not having the (powerful, terrifying) motivation to get paid or die trying. |

## Having Wealth

If John Hughes, Rupert Murdoch, and Bill Gates could agree on one thing, it'd be a tie between "malaria is bad" and "being rich makes it soooo much easier to get laid." On the other hand, if we can learn anything from slimy James Spader in *Pretty in Pink*, Murdoch's string of ex-wives, and Gates's ability to find a steady partner able to ignore his haircut, it's that money might be able to get you dates, but unless you're smart (about everything but how to choose a barber), it can prevent you from getting dates that you can trust, connect with, or do anything but spoil and perhaps resent. That's because wealth shapes others' expectations, as well as yours, in ways that interfere with friendship, mutual respect, and even having a good time. Instead of holding out hope for a spark that makes all the wealth-related prejudices and reflexes melt away, learn what to expect from others and develop methods for managing their attitudes. Then you can know whether someone likes you for you and not just for your parents' giant house or media empire or philanthropic fortune and the chance you'll go bald.

Here are three examples:

- *I didn't grow up in a mansion or anything, but my family was wealthy, and now that I've achieved some professional success myself, I'm fairly well-off. I try not to be ostentatious or flaunt what I have, but when I start dating someone and she finds out that I do have some money, it always causes problems. She either thinks I'm judging her for having less money (I'm not) or that my having money means I'm an asshole (I'm not, I hope). My goal is to find someone who doesn't think the worst of me once she finds out I'm not broke.*

- *I'm not a repulsive man, but I know that my most attractive quality isn't my face. I'm extremely successful, and I'm not ashamed of it, but I'm also not looking to be with someone who only sees me as a fat bank account. Because I work hard for my success, I don't have a lot of time to meet women, and that makes it even more frustrating when the women who want to meet me are only interested in my net worth. My goal is to find a woman who doesn't care about my wealth.*

• *I grew up with money, but I don't have much any more now that*
*I'm grown-up and I'm not good at making it, so I've realized I*
*need a man who is financially successful. I wish it weren't this way*
*because it makes me feel shallow, but I can't support any guy I'm*
*with and I don't want to live less comfortably than I'm used to.*
*My goal is to find someone nice who is also reasonably wealthy,*
*without feeling guilty about it, so I can return to the kind of*
*lifestyle I've always been accustomed to.*

Unlike a sense of humor, family, brains, and many other qualities described in this book, wealth isn't a permanent part, or even necessarily a reflection, of who somebody is. Sure, wealth is desirable, can shape a person's character, and be as inherited as your mother's comic timing or your father's love of reading historical biographies; unlike those things, however, wealth can be impermanent, impersonal, and a sometimes unimportant indicator of someone's true nature.

As discussed earlier, seeking someone with resources isn't unwise or superficial, but if you are wealthy and judged only by those resources, money becomes a barrier to finding a partner instead of a shortcut. So, when one person has more than the other, building chemistry based on character and discovering whether that chemistry makes for genuine compatibility requires extra work and patience.

People who come from old money—the kind that goes back generations, not that has cobwebs on it or lives in the old-Krugerrand home—often notice the negative feelings their wealth arouses when they date outside their economic and social class. Whether envious or not or whether their prejudices are deserved or not, people are quick to assume that wealthy people, especially those raised with wealth, are spoiled, lazy monsters who hire personal assistants for their cats and limit their work to that on their tans at beachfront estates in St. Barts. So, if you're wealthy and wish to date outside your social class, you will probably run into negative judgments you don't deserve, and it's natural to become defensive and frustrated when that dating is more difficult than you expected.

It won't help to hide or apologize for your wealth or to worry too much about how it will be perceived. Instead, review your spending priorities and practices and determine for yourself whether what you do with money reflects values you believe in, such as education, self-reliance, and being a good friend and family member. The more confident you are in your money management, not simply in profit making (but not excluding it, either), the more you can share your wealth-related activities with a prospective partner as if you're sharing a part of who you are, not what you were born into.

As long as you're comfortable that your spending decisions reflect your personality and moral priorities, you can use wealth as a screening tool. Those who can't see past their negative feelings or prejudice about money are never going to be real friends, but those who respect what you're doing with your money, as you do, can respect the real you and be the kind of friends and partners that last.

If you're particularly good at making money, it's hard to escape the false attractiveness that draws supermodels, supersycophants, and the generally shallow. Even people who don't intend to be gold diggers find themselves attracted to and impressed with financial success, and since working takes up most of your time, that is bound to make the screening and searching of dating a lot more difficult.

One way to use wealth to make dating easier is to hire a match-maker. Yes, they exist in real life, and unlike the worn leather sack filled with rabid possums who does the job on Bravo, good match-makers do the detective work and commonsense screening that we advise people to do for themselves. There's nothing wrong with delegating, particularly if you're using an experienced, not-sack-based professional who helps you approach the task the way a head-hunter would help you find a coexecutive.

Write a job description and the criteria for skills, education, background, and personality traits that you think are necessary. Keep in mind your availability, or lack of it; you obviously need someone who is sufficiently independent not to resent your work commitment. Even if you don't feel comfortable working with a match-maker, don't let financial success turn you into a lonely prince of commerce. If you use your wealth and business acumen to streamline the search, you've got a good chance of filling your partnership position.

If you've grown up with wealth but then grow out of it and discover you have no talent for making it on your own, looking for someone with money may seem like the best way to secure your return to the class you consider home. While there's nothing shallow about wanting and needing material comfort, especially if it's the only kind of life you've ever known, it can be dangerous to let financial neediness lower your standards, weaken your evaluation of a rich man's character, and blind you to flaws, faults, and incompatibilities that will prevent you from developing a real, respectful partnership.

Unless you're particularly mercenary and insensitive, winning a rich partner will hurt you as much as him when you find yourselves bound to someone you don't like or trust. So, instead of wasting time with guilt and self-doubt, take extra care getting to know a wealthy potential partner until you're as sure of his character and your mutual affection as you are of his pocketbook. Yes, it's easier to evaluate a partnership candidate when you're not feeling needy, but life doesn't offer you that choice. So rely on your experience, be extra careful, and trust your ability to get to know someone and develop a real relationship, even when distracted by financial need.

Having wealth may be good for your ego, sense of security, and your cat's PA, but it doesn't make finding or developing a good relationship any easier. Wealth can become more of an asset to your search than an obstacle, however, if you use it as a reflection of your good character or as a tool to find someone worthwhile. The dating pool is the great equalizer in that everybody, rich and poor alike, is required to learn the basics of what they need and conduct a search according to carefully developed standards. Do that, and wealth won't prevent you from finding someone who accepts and loves you for who you are, not what you've got.

## Too Motivated by Money?

Red flags that you're on a first date with someone who's way too fixated on finances:

- He refuses to ride to the restaurant in your trusted old Toyota since he doesn't get into cars that are older than the fancy cheese in his fridge and more embarrassing than the experimental Danish anti-hair-loss ointment he keeps next to it.
- After noticing the cumulative classiness of your watch, car, and address, he rejects your offer to treat him to a movie for your second date and suggests you instead treat him to a weeklong getaway in Bermuda.
- Says she'd love to meet up for coffee once she gets some fundamental information, e.g., the coffee shop address, a description of what you'll be wearing, and copies of your last three months of bank statements.
- After you assure him that you are, in fact, treating him to dinner at what is his favorite restaurant, he orders six entrées and calls his roommate to ask what he'd like for dinner this week since some sucker is buying and you're not sharing your shrimp risotto.

> • You assumed he wanted to meet for an early dinner because he had plans later, but you discover it was so he could catch the early-bird special *and* ride his bike there and back while it was still light out, when it's easier to see and collect soda cans by the side of the road. You correctly assume he's not paying for dinner.

## Wealth and Marriage

Even if you're a die-hard romantic and still believe, after all these pages, that love must be at the core of any good marriage, you have to acknowledge that money is at the core of almost all marital arguments. And if a fight isn't directly about money, it's usually only a few degrees of separation away from it; after all, money, not love, is necessary to a family's survival and growth, forces you to make tough decisions, and, if you have kids, always seems to be in short supply. You might think that, if you had enough wealth, you wouldn't have to worry about survival, hard choices, or arguments, but no amount of money can buy you out of marital conflict because there are always reasonable and meaningful options that cost more money, and the more those options cost, the more important they are. So making decisions about money—the making, spending, saving, sharing, and prioritizing of it—is, in a way, what marriage is about. You can be rich in love, but if you're poor in funds, your marriage may still end up broke.

Here are three examples:

- *My wife and I had a successful business for a long time that provided us with a comfortable lifestyle, but then our industry went bust and we suddenly find ourselves hustling in the job market, looking for a smaller place to rent, and turning down invitations to dine at unaffordable restaurants with friends who*

*eventually stop returning our calls. My wife and I are holding
on to each other for dear life, wondering if we can survive this
transition, hoping we can do so with our marriage intact. My goal
is to protect my marriage despite my being angry, scared, and
feeling like a failure.*

- *I felt like Cinderella when I married a smart, creative guy with
a big trust fund, and I liked that our family would be secure
while he pursued his interests. The trouble is that he's never found
anything that's grabbed him for more than a year or two. If he's
not so entranced with something that he's relatively unavailable,
then he's around all the time and depressed until he finds
something new. I'm pretty happy raising the kids, but ten years
into our marriage, he's still drifting and restless. My goal is to have
a relationship with my husband that I can count on (or just a
reliable husband, period).*

- *I feel I made a bad deal with my marriage, and I can't help
resenting my husband. He's a nice guy with a good heart and an
excellent job, so I married him, even though I didn't love him,
because I knew he'd be a good dad and a reliable partner, and I
didn't think I'd find someone better. Plus my parents married for
love and my family was broke and miserable, so I thought it was
a small sacrifice. My husband's all that I thought he'd be and we
have a lovely home, but I find myself resenting him more and
more as the years go by. It's not his fault or anything he's doing
specifically, it's just the small things that I find irritating, that
maybe I wouldn't find so irritating if I'd loved him more in the
first place. So I feel bad about putting him down, hurting the
kids, and being a jerk. My goal is to stop hurting him but stay
married.*

The simplest way to look at how wealth factors into a marriage is to see it as the fuel that gets your marriage-mobile to where you need it to go; if you want to have enough food or take a vacation or get the kids to private school, money is what makes all of that possible. Shared values, beliefs, and goals are what build the vehicle, and maybe, to paraphrase the film *Serenity*, love is what keeps it on the road, but without fuel, it will get stuck, and then there's no guarantee you won't end up hitchhiking off in separate directions.

Of the many factors that can impact your family's wealth, luck is a major one, and suddenly losing money (and the friends, social standing, and lifestyle that go with it) is one of the toughest challenges a marriage can endure besides severe illness and moving in with your in-laws on their houseboat. While nobody can control luck, your response to that financial luck (or lack thereof) is not only within your control, it's also a measure of your character, both as an individual and as a family comanager.

Loss of wealth naturally prompts you to wonder what you did wrong, who's responsible, and what you should have done differently. The more severe the loss, the broader its impact on where you live, what you can do for your kids, and how you spend time with friends. The deeper your ties to a community and your commitment to raising children, the more it hurts. That's why losing wealth feels like the essence of failure, and if you make the mistake of believing those feelings, failure becomes reality. Feelings of failure drive you to withdraw, stop working or looking for work, blame your partner, yell at the kids, possibly drink too much, and become everything you don't respect. They are infectious and can demoralize everyone in the family, including your partner, kids, and pets.

What you must accept is that financial loss is an unavoidable part of life and that what counts is what you do with it. Yes, you may have made stupid mistakes or be bad with money, and daily events, along

with your spouse and kids, may provide you with regular remind-
ers of the impact of your loss. Don't make it worse by holding yourself responsible for your pain. Instead, judge your situation as you
would a friend's, giving yourself the benefit of the doubt and thinking constructively instead of focusing on blame; refuse to crimi-
nalize stupid mistakes or assume that guilt and suffering should be
proportionate to how much pain results from that mistake.

Decisions that turn out badly are not necessarily mistakes, but if
you actually did something wrong, remember that your goal isn't to
self-flagellate, but to do better. Once you've learned what you can and
apologized if necessary, begin living with the luck you have. Success
is not measured by how well you maintain or restore family wealth,
but by how well, despite humiliation and loss, you stand by your values, continue to work hard, and do your job as a partner and parent.

Many of those who grow up with wealth, spared from the conflicts and challenges of life's regular tasks, can feel bored and insignificant, obliging them to find a creative calling to make their lives
meaningful. In marrying such a person, you think you've lucked out
by acquiring both financial security for your family and a special
kind of companionship that is more interesting and available than
that offered by someone forced to make a regular living.

The danger is that if your spouse takes the ordinary responsibilities of partnership and parenting for granted and overvalues creativity, he can focus too much on his dreams and not on the day to
day. Marrying a dreamer may seem romantic, but nothing about
being bound to an unreliable, self-centered asshole is romantic,
even if the bills are always paid. He's not necessarily malicious, but
in his own genial, princely way he feels entitled to flee boredom and
pursue whatever and whoever is new and interesting, regardless of
prior commitments or responsibilities. If that's the kind of guy you
married, you're in trouble.

If you complain or urge him to stand by his family commitments, he is likely to withdraw while acting as if you're trying to push him into depression and banal captivity. He'll tell his shrink, if he sees one, that you've turned into precisely the needy, demanding, conventional partner he was determined to avoid and you promised not to be. Even if the therapist seems sympathetic to your point of view, the therapist won't get any further than you since your spouse just won't show up again.

Instead of complaining, remind your husband how much you respect whatever he contributes as companion and parent, even when the job is irritating and boring. Discuss his unhappiness as something that may be inevitable, particularly if he is prone to depression, and that his unhappiness doesn't signify to you that he hasn't found his calling in life or that he's an unsuccessful human being. Urge him to relieve symptoms of depression with treatment, if that's what his lethargy and uneasiness truly are, and to learn to tolerate unhappiness without necessarily questioning the meaning of his life goals.

Hopefully, he can respond to your good advice. If not, you've done your best to help him settle down, and now it's time to stop taking responsibility for his unhappiness, build up your independence, and carefully evaluate whether this marriage is worth holding together for you and your kids. If it is, respect the extra work required to manage a family as an unequally partnered parent, and if it isn't, respect yourself for making a difficult choice.

Despite what films, country songs, and human-interest stories on the news about happily married centenarians say, many people marry without ever feeling madly in love. Having suffered breakups and breakdowns with previous, well-loved partners who couldn't do their share, manage money, or stay faithful, lots of people are just happy to find someone they can trust, respect, and work with reliably and without drama. In most cases, love grows, even if it's never mad or doesn't stay deeply passionate for longer than the life span of a parrot.

If you're unlucky, however, and find yourself increasingly irritated with a perfectly nice husband, it's hard not to feel guilty when there's everything to like and you just can't get yourself to feel the way you should. That guilt makes you more irritated, and irritation makes you feel guilty, and on it goes. You wish you could work out your issues and feel comfortable and happy with a guy who's a good match, but what you learn is that no one controls his or her feelings, with or without therapy, so making yourself feel more love or just less guilt isn't in the cards.

So don't dwell on your failure to feel the way you should. Instead, review the advantages of staying married such as your finances, the kids' security, and having a good working relationship with your husband. If the advantages outweigh your unhappiness, respect yourself for tolerating the painful chemistry of your marriage for a worthwhile cause, and work hard to find distracting hobbies, such as running or volunteering, to keep your mind on something besides your irritating spouse.

If it's no longer worth staying, don't overapologize for feelings you could never help, but do express regret for a good partnership that ran into bad luck. Take credit for the good family you built together, then reclaim your single life and commence a search that's still pragmatic but with more of an emphasis on finding a partner who provides more support than irritation. You can't assume that your mistake was to overrate money or underrate love, rather than to overrate your ability to control your emotions.

Having wealth in a marriage opens the door for many worthwhile life goals and can reduce certain sources of marital conflict, but it can also foster overdependence on and overvaluation of lifestyle goals that are not important and become a false measure of success. Remember, wealth is the gas, which means it can take you far even if your marriage-mobile is otherwise in need of repair and at risk of exploding at any minute. So don't measure your marriage based on the destination, but on how you manage, or survive, the journey.

## Did You Know . . . Truth, or Bullshit?

*We examine widely accepted beliefs about relationships to determine whether they're true (or not so much). The phrase in question:*
"You'll find someone the minute you stop looking."

Usually, if you're trying to achieve a difficult personal goal, be it getting a new job, quitting cigarettes, or finding a vintage PJ Harvey T-shirt on eBay for under $200, being driven is a good thing. When you're looking for a partner, however, being driven can sometimes read as being needy, and if you seem too desperate, you'll end up scaring potential partners away or accepting unworthy ones out of sheer determination to reach that relationship target. You're especially at risk if your desperation pushes you to compromise your standards and give any willing biped a chance. In these instances, this saying is true: if you're not actively looking, your choices won't be warped by neediness, and you may actually find someone you wouldn't if you were actively on the hunt.

On the other hand, if you have no eligible partners in a situation—e.g., if most people your age have already paired off, or your tastes are a little unconventional, or you're a single woman in New York City (but not Staten Island)—you won't find someone unless you *are* determined, because you'll need to look hard and with great care. If you aren't looking at all, you won't be avoiding losers, you'll be avoiding the search and the possibility for partnership altogether.

Plus, people often invoke the "not looking is the best policy" dictum after too many bad dates and attempts at finding someone worthwhile have left them with a bad case of burnout (and nothing more if they're lucky or used protection). Not looking becomes synonymous with giving up, ignoring the burnout, and pretending that you're still looking when you're really in a committed relationship with Netflix and your couch. The smarter option isn't to stop looking, but to look for better guys by toughening up your criteria. That way you can stop wasting time on bad candidates and protect yourself from burning out and bingeing on *Lady Dynamite* in one sitting.

While it is true that you will find something meaningful with someone when you aren't desperate enough to accept anything that's moving, it's not true that you'll find someone if you entirely lose the will to search. So, no, you won't necessarily find someone when you aren't looking, but you will find someone good for you if you aren't looking for any old moron with a pulse.

VERDICT: TRUE-ISH SOMETIMES, BUT FREQUENTLY BULLSHIT

The financial potential of a partnership is important for the security of anyone who wants kids, to be able to send those kids to college, or just wants to keep themselves and/or their kids from a career redeeming bottles and cans. While extreme wealth doesn't guarantee you can keep a marriage together—just ask the British royal family—few partnerships last if they make one or both parties substantially poorer. That's why how one responds to the stress of gaining or losing wealth, not the problems money solves, is the best indicator of the potential strength of your union. Those moments tell you how strong a person is and what he can contribute when bad luck arrives, which it always does. Don't feel guilty or superficial for caring about how much money you need a partner to have, but it's more important to know whether a partner's values are strong enough to stand up to the sooner-or-later stress of financial fluc-tuations. If he or she has that strength, then God save this possible king or queen.

| What to Look For | What to Achieve/What Not to Be Fooled By |
| --- | --- |
| Mutual attraction | . . . based on each other's ability to save and prioritize spending, not on having the ability to blow cash on fine wines, five-star hotels, and foolish, great expectations. |
| Mutual respect | . . . for what you accomplished when there wasn't much money to go around, and not for what you spent it on when you got a lucky fistful of dollars or a family fortune. |
| Shared effort | . . . on working hard, deciding together what's most worth saving for, and then finding ways to have fun together, rather than in finding new ways to feel better by spending more without worrying about tomorrow. |
| Common interests | . . . in what you like to save for, spend on, and donate to, rather than in climbing a social ladder to gain self-esteem. |
| Common goals | . . . to make enough money for survival, security, and building a family and a strong foundation for your kids in the future, not for buying yourself into the 1 percent and the good feelings that go with it. |

## Should My Partner and I Have a Baby?

Congratulations! Not because you're having a baby, but because you're smart enough to think twice about having a kid, which already shows great parenthood potential. Before deciding to become a parent, you have lots of important factors to consider, starting with how experienced you and your partner are with kids, and whether any experience indicates potential parenthood red flags. The timing also has to be considered, as well as you and your partner's abilities to take on the many massive sacrifices and tough choices that parenthood entails. If you come through this evaluation feeling confident that you, your partner, and your relationship have what it takes to make a family, then congratulations for real. If you instead discover that you currently don't have the experience, resources, and/or sturdy partnership that parenthood requires—and remember, babies don't solve problems between couples, they open up an entire universe of new ones—then congratulations for making a smart but difficult choice, and for having learned what you'll need to make parenthood a better option in the future.

**Warning:**

This chart assumes that you have cleared three of the biggest hurdles to making this decision and are thus:

1. Free of fertility issues;

2. At an age where you couldn't have a baby in a pact with your homeroom besties or to get onto *Teen Mom*;

3. Not already being told by everyone in your life and/or time traveling rebels in the future war against Skynet that this is a really bad idea.

   Otherwise, as they say in the world of grant writing, *if you do not qualify, do not apply,* which is to say, skip this quiz and get your egg or sperm count checked, or wait to finish high school, or listen to John Connor because otherwise, like raising a baby when you're not equipped, your future is fucked.

**Key**

| Our Question |
| --- |

| Your answers in the "yes" family |
| --- |

| Your answers in the "no" family |
| --- |

To Conclusion: ━━━━━━

# Should My Partner and I Have a Baby?

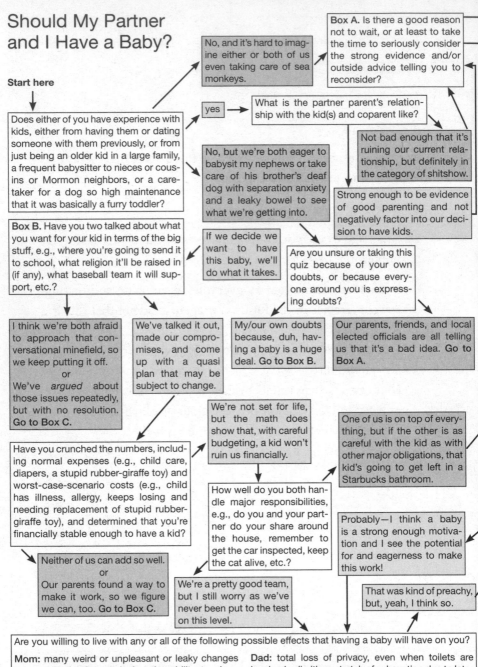

**Start here**

Does either of you have experience with kids, either from having them or dating someone with them previously, or from just being an older kid in a large family, a frequent babysitter to nieces or cousins or Mormon neighbors, or a caretaker for a dog so high maintenance that it was basically a furry toddler?

No, and it's hard to imagine either or both of us even taking care of sea monkeys.

yes

What is the partner parent's relationship with the kid(s) and coparent like?

**Box A.** Is there a good reason not to wait, or at least to take the time to seriously consider the strong evidence and/or outside advice telling you to reconsider?

Not bad enough that it's ruining our current relationship, but definitely in the category of shitshow.

No, but we're both eager to babysit my nephews or take care of his brother's deaf dog with separation anxiety and a leaky bowel to see what we're getting into.

Strong enough to be evidence of good parenting and not negatively factor into our decision to have kids.

**Box B.** Have you two talked about what you want for your kid in terms of the big stuff, e.g., where you're going to send it to school, what religion it'll be raised in (if any), what baseball team it will support, etc.?

If we decide we want to have this baby, we'll do what it takes.

Are you unsure or taking this quiz because of your own doubts, or because everyone around you is expressing doubts?

I think we're both afraid to approach that conversational minefield, so we keep putting it off.
or
We've *argued* about those issues repeatedly, but with no resolution. **Go to Box C.**

We've talked it out, made our compromises, and come up with a quasi plan that may be subject to change.

My/our own doubts because, duh, having a baby is a huge deal. **Go to Box B.**

Our parents, friends, and local elected officials are all telling us that it's a bad idea. **Go to Box A.**

Have you crunched the numbers, including normal expenses (e.g., child care, diapers, a stupid rubber-giraffe toy) and worst-case-scenario costs (e.g., child has illness, allergy, keeps losing and needing replacement of stupid rubber-giraffe toy), and determined that you're financially stable enough to have a kid?

We're not set for life, but the math does show that, with careful budgeting, a kid won't ruin us financially.

One of us is on top of everything, but if the other is as careful with the kid as with other major obligations, that kid's going to get left in a Starbucks bathroom.

How well do you both handle major responsibilities, e.g., do you and your partner do your share around the house, remember to get the car inspected, keep the cat alive, etc.?

Probably—I think a baby is a strong enough motivation and I see the potential for and eagerness to make this work!

Neither of us can add so well.
or
Our parents found a way to make it work, so we figure we can, too. **Go to Box C.**

We're a pretty good team, but I still worry as we've never been put to the test on this level.

That was kind of preachy, but, yeah, I think so.

Are you willing to live with any or all of the following possible effects that having a baby will have on you?

**Mom:** many weird or unpleasant or leaky changes to your body; forever losing the ability to sleep soundly without chemical assistance; and having to constantly nag your husband to watch or play with or wipe the kids because you're far more alert to the kids' needs than he is?

**Dad:** total loss of privacy, even when toilets are involved; a limitless stretch of exhaustion due to late-night feedings or peed beds or sleepless nights wondering how you'll pay for your kid's braces; having your wife nag you to do things for the kids because she has a weird sixth sense for when they need to eat or be changed or get yelled at and you don't?

**Yes, you should have a baby.** Lucky for you, your trepidations about parenthood are a reflection of your strong understanding of how much work and responsibility parenting requires, not any obvious signs that you and your partner will be unable to fulfill those obligations. There's never a sure sign that the time is right to have a kid, and there's no way to guarantee that your kid will be happy, healthy, and not a serial killer, but based on your answers, you have plenty of good reasons to believe that you won't be taking an unreasonable risk by becoming a parent.

Since he doesn't like condoms and I don't like abortion, the question isn't whether we're having the baby, but whether we're raising it together. Go to Box B.

No, except that I loooooove him.
or
*Me wantee baby.*
or
We might break up otherwise.

**Maybe you should have a baby.** Ideally, you'd push through a lot more difficult conversations with your partner before deciding to have a kid. That way you both can be sure you're doing the right thing before committing to parenthood and a possible lifetime of the exact kind of arguments you're desperate to avoid right now. If waiting is not an option, brace yourself for tough times as a couple from the stress of either a subpar, half-baked parenting team or a tough road to conception. Prepare for the possibilities that your relationship may not survive and you may end up raising a kid on your own or that you may be unable to have a kid at all.

Crappy coparent, fuckup for life!. Go to Box C.

Do you think having a baby would successfully force the flakier partner to learn the time-management techniques required to get his or her shit together, or do you think a baby would only make that partner more distant and unwilling to change his or her ways and you'd end up with a crappy coparent?

From all that I see and my partner says, yes, indeed.

If your partner can't pull it together, are you determined enough to have a kid that you'd be okay with doing the majority of the parenting, whether or not you go through a divorce and custody battle (but especially if you do)?

If my relationship can't survive our kid, so be it.

As much as I want a kid, I want my marriage more.

And are you sure your partner's willing to do the same?

If I'm being honest . . .

Maybe . . . or not . . . care to elaborate?

**Box C.** If you're not willing to resolve or even discuss this issue before the baby comes, are you willing to accept that, once the baby's here, you'll need to make all the sacrifices required to resolve the issue, make parenting work, and put your kid first?

Ugh . . . that sounds like hard work, which is my least favorite thing next to caring and forgetting to buy more vape juice.

**No, you shouldn't have a baby.** No matter what your hormones, heart, or friends in homeroom may be telling you, do right by yourself, your partner, and some future parole officer and do not have a kid right now, or maybe ever. Remember, you can have a happy relationship, and a full life, without adding a child to the mix. Lots of people aren't built for parenthood, so don't feel like a failure or a freak if having a kid isn't ultimately in the cards. For now, the possibility of your becoming a parent is a losing hand for everyone, so keep using birth control and improve your common sense.

I . . . uh . . . help!

# Acknowledgments

## Both Bennetts:

As always, we're grateful to our agent, Anthony Mattero; our editor, Trish Todd; her right hand, Kaitlin Olson; and the entire FF Inc./Touchstone team: Susan Moldow, Tara Parsons, David Falk, Meredith Vilarello, Kelsey Manning, Shida Carr, Erich Hobbing, Cherlynne Li, and copyeditors Navorn Johnson and Steve Boldt (for teaching us that "fuckup" is one word). Thanks also to S&S press wizards Amanda Lang and Ebony LaDelle and radio guru Chuck Monroe. Thanks also to our online ambassador, Madison Cleo.

Thank you to every press outlet—radio station, magazine, carrier pigeon—that helped promote our first book. This may seem like a craven plea for more attention, but really it's an attempt to alleviate the guilt of forgetting grandma's advice and not writing "thank you" notes in a timely manner.

Thanks again/always to legal consigliere Quinn Heraty, who begat working with Liz Gallagher, Candace Kreinbrink, and Anthony. Thank you all for believing in us and being so great.

We're still grateful to daughter/sister Rebecca, son-/brother-in-law

Aaron, and their litter of children. And really to all the family members (both official and otherwise) in Massachusetts, Vermont, New Jersey, New York, New Hampshire, Florida, Ontario, England, etc., whom we never get to see enough of but who don't get annoyed when we do see them and tell the same four stories about Grandma all over again.

Special thanks to our old friend Dr. Nancy Cotton for her autism expertise and for donning a Teletubby costume in public. Thanks also to her children: Anna, for her keen interest in our work from the get-go; Mary, who also works with autistic kids and first introduced Sarah to the "social fake" concept (for which Sarah's grateful whenever she has to be, ugh, social); and Billy, who is gifted with extraordinary social and design skills. Thanks also to father/husband Dr. Paul Cotton, as we fear his wrath if he's left out.

Thank you, Eudora Prescod, who taught us that mockery can be a sincere form of affection.

We'll thank Dr. Mona Bennett again, on top of the dedication. It's the right thing to do, dammit.

We're still not okay with thanking each other, though. It's weird.

**Michael:**

Thanks to Mel Brooks, Don Rickles, and Louis Black, who taught me more about the therapeutic impact of curmudgeonly corrections than the entire collected works of Sigmund Freud.

This book also owes much to my failed relationships and partnerships. Often, what went wrong could only be helped by going back in time, recognizing what couldn't work, and building acceptance into future choices.

The ideas in this book emerged during conversations with patients about their experiences with love, loss, and relationships, and are as much theirs as mine.

And thank you to my social-worker sister, Naomi, for still talking to me after we mocked her profession in our first book (that after an entire childhood of torment).

And a special thanks to my old boss, Dr. Jon Gudeman, who gave me the idea for an op-ed piece thirty years ago; I actually got to write it for the *New York Times* last year but only recently realized that the original idea was his. Please accept my gratitude, apologies, and an imaginary byline.


***Sarah:***

Thank to all my exes, unrequited crushes, and basically every guy whose name I bothered to learn but who was still a dick to me. Your collective shittiness netted me a book's worth of jokes (and some rare LPs), so I guess it was worth it.

Thank you to the following people I don't know, but whose work and contribution to the universe/my life filled my heart with love during the writing process: David Ortiz (David Ortiz! David Ortiz!), Don Orsillo, HRM HRC, Ronna & Beverly, Joss Whedon, Pamela Adlon, Maira Kalman, Jen Kirkman, Amy Sherman-Palladino, and, of course, Prince.

Thank you, Maria Bamford, who was so kind to me when we met that I still think it was all a hallucination.

Big thanks to Leah Tamburino, makeup artist, and Paul Ferraro, hairstylist, at *CBS This Morning*. These two wizards didn't just make me look TV-pretty, they basically pulled a full-on *Face/Off*, and while I have since returned to my original, Nicolas Cage state, their miraculous efforts are not forgotten.

Extra thanks to Navorn Johnson and Erich Hobbing for their help with the flowcharts (and sorry for creating yet more work for you by adding this last-minute acknowledgment).

Since my beloved dog, Avon Barksdale, cannot read, thank you to Peace and Paws Dog Rescue (peaceandpaws.org) of Hillsborough, New Hampshire, for bringing him into my life and, in doing so, teaching me to love again. And thanks to petfinder.org, which led me to Peace and Paws, as well as to the dog jail in Meriden, Connecticut, where I found my first dog and first real love, King Buzzo (zt"l).

Thanks again to every single friend and family member I thanked in the first book, most of whom I do really, truly love in one way or another (most "like family," a few "like Fresca"). Special thanks to old friends Kathleen Billus, who first taught me about the permaflirt (then known as Roboflirt) and is still my friend after all the years and all my recent work-related neglect (and even after all the unbelievable horseshit she's had to deal with in general); Lizzy Castruccio Kim, who has suffered just as much neglect on top of the loss of Vin Scully; Bill and Eilene Russell, who only get my full attention during spring training and if there's a Sonic Drive-In nearby; Dr. Rebecca Onion, who gave my father his first gig with published advice back at *YM* and was extra helpful when it came to putting together the pain-in-the-*tuchus* charts in this book; and Emma Forrest, who hustled so hard to get me blurbs for book #1 despite her already full, top-notch hustlin' schedule. And of course, huge thanks to the only friend dedicated and loving enough to stand by my side always, especially and literally at a show that featured both Morrissey *and* Danzig, Maysan Haydar (and all Haydars everywhere).

# Index

## About the Authors

Dr. Michael I. Bennett, educated at both Harvard College and Harvard Medical School, is a board-certified psychiatrist, a Canadian, and a Red Sox fan. While he's worked in every aspect of his field from hospital administration to managed care, his major interest is his private practice, which he's been running for almost thirty years. The author of *F*ck Feelings* with his daughter Sarah Bennett, he lives with his wife in Boston and New Hampshire.

Sarah Bennett has written for magazines, the Internet, television, and books. She also spent two years writing for a monthly sketch comedy show at the Upright Citizens Brigade Theater in New York City. When not living by her philosophy of "will write for food," Sarah walks her dog, watches Red Sox games, and avoids eye contact with other humans. Somehow, she lives in New Hampshire and works in New York.